MASTERING DIGITAL MARKETING SUCCESSFULLY

FROM THE BASICS TO THE EXPERT LEVEL – STRATEGIES, TECHNIQUES AND TRENDS FOR A SUCCESSFUL ONLINE PRESENCE

Ethan Clarke

TABLE OF CONTENTS

Introduction to Digital Marketing 5
   What is digital marketing? 5
   Why is digital marketing important? 8
   The Evolution of Digital Marketing 10
   The Benefits of Digital Marketing..13

The Basics of Digital Marketing 16
   Target group analysis..16
   The Marketing Strategy 18
   Choosing the right channels 21
   Measuring success in digital marketing.......................................25

Search Engine Optimization (SEO)..29
   Basics of Search Engine Optimization 29
   Keyword Research & Optimization 31
   On-Page Optimization 35
   Off-Page Optimization 38
   Technical SEO Optimization..41
   SEO Tools & Trends 44

Search Engine Marketing (SEM) 48
   Basics of Search Engine Marketing..48
   Google Ads and other ad networks...51
   Keyword-Advertising 54
   Display Advertising..57
   Remarketing und Retargeting 61

Social Media Marketing 66
   The Importance of Social Media in Marketing 66
   Choosing the Right Social Media Platforms 69

Content strategy for social media 72

Community Management & Customer Engagement.......................76

Content Marketing...81

Fundamentals of Content Marketing 81

Content Strategy & Planning...84

Content Creation & Distribution 88

Content Optimization & Measurement...............................92

Email marketing and newsletters...96

Email marketing as an effective marketing tool...............96

Building an email list and segmentation.........................99

Create and send email campaigns...................................101

Measuring and optimising success in email marketing 104

Mobile Marketing & App Marketing 109

The Importance of Mobile Marketing 109

Mobile optimization of websites and apps 111

App Marketing Strategies..114

App Store Optimization (ASO) 118

Mobile Ad Networks and Formats 120

INTRODUCTION TO DIGITAL MARKETING

WHAT IS DIGITAL MARKETING?

Digital marketing, also known as online marketing or internet marketing, refers to all marketing activities that are carried out through digital channels. It involves using various online platforms, such as websites, search engines, social media, emails, and mobile apps, to promote products and services and reach customers.

THE IMPORTANCE OF DIGITAL MARKETING

In an increasingly digitized world, digital marketing is crucial for businesses to connect with their target audience and increase their brand awareness. Compared to traditional marketing methods, digital marketing offers a number of advantages that make it more effective and cost-effective.

THE BENEFITS OF DIGITAL MARKETING

Greater reach and target group targeting

Digital marketing allows businesses to communicate their message to a wider audience. By using online channels, they can reach potential customers all over the world. In addition, digital marketing makes it possible to target specific target groups. By analyzing data, companies can tailor their marketing strategies to the needs and interests of their target audience and deliver personalized content.

Measurability and success monitoring

Unlike traditional marketing methods, digital marketing provides an opportunity to accurately measure and analyze the success of a campaign. Companies can use analytics tools to collect and evaluate data about the performance of their marketing activities. This allows them to better understand the return on investment (ROI) of their marketing spend and optimize their strategies.

Cost effectiveness

Digital marketing is usually more cost-effective than traditional marketing. Companies can use their marketing budgets more efficiently by investing in online channels that offer greater reach and better targeting. Compared to print ads or television commercials, digital marketing campaigns can be run at a fraction of the cost.

Interactive communication and customer loyalty

Digital marketing enables direct and interactive communication with customers. Businesses can connect with their customers through social media, emails, or chatbots and respond to their questions and concerns. By building a strong online presence and providing high-quality content, businesses can build customer engagement and brand loyalty.

Flexibility and adaptability

Digital marketing offers businesses the opportunity to quickly adapt their marketing strategies and respond to current trends and changes in the market. Compared to traditional marketing methods, digital marketing campaigns can be created and implemented in less time. Businesses can update their messages and offers in real-time, maintaining their relevance to the target audience.

THE EVOLUTION OF DIGITAL MARKETING

Digital marketing has evolved a lot over the years. It used to be mostly limited to emails and websites, but today there are a variety of channels and technologies available. The increasing prevalence of smartphones and the growing importance of social media have further driven digital marketing.

The evolution of digital marketing goes hand-in-hand with technological advancements. New tools and platforms are continuously being developed to help businesses implement their marketing strategies. Artificial intelligence, machine learning, and big data are playing an increasingly important role in digital marketing, as they help businesses analyze data and create personalized marketing campaigns.

RESULT

Digital marketing is an essential part of modern marketing. It provides companies with the opportunity to effectively target their target audience, increase their brand awareness, and measure the success of their marketing efforts. By leveraging various online channels and technologies, businesses can adapt their marketing strategies and strengthen their customer loyalty. In the following chapters, we will take a closer look at the basics of digital marketing, such as audience analysis, marketing strategy, and choosing the right channels.

WHY IS DIGITAL MARKETING IMPORTANT?

In today's digital world, marketing through the internet and other digital channels is vital to the success of a business. Digital marketing offers numerous benefits and opportunities that traditional marketing methods cannot. In this section, we'll take a closer look at the importance of digital marketing and why it's essential for businesses.

ACCESSIBILITY OF A BROAD TARGET GROUP

A major advantage of digital marketing is the ability to reach a wide audience. Unlike traditional marketing methods, which are often limited to a specific geographic region, digital marketing allows businesses to target customers all over the world. By leveraging various digital channels such as websites, social media, and email marketing, businesses can send their message to potential customers in different countries and regions. This opens up new opportunities for companies to grow their business and enter new markets.

EFFECTIVE TARGETING AND PERSONALIZATION

Digital marketing allows businesses to effectively reach their target audience and tailor their marketing messages to individual needs and interests. By using data analytics and tracking tools, businesses can better understand their customers' behavior and preferences and create personalized content and offers. This leads to greater relevance of marketing messages and better customer loyalty. By targeting their target audience accurately, companies can use their marketing budgets more efficiently and achieve better results.

MEASURABILITY AND ANALYSIS

Another important aspect of digital marketing is the ability to accurately measure and analyze the success of marketing campaigns. Unlike traditional marketing methods, where it is difficult to determine the exact success of a campaign, digital marketing offers a variety of tools and metrics to measure success. Businesses can track exactly how many people have seen their ads, how many clicks they've received, and how many conversions they've generated. This data allows companies to continuously optimize their marketing strategies and achieve better results.

COST SAVINGS

Digital marketing offers businesses the opportunity to significantly reduce their marketing costs. Compared to traditional marketing methods such as print advertising or television commercials, digital marketing channels are often more cost-effective and offer a better return on the money invested. Companies can use their marketing budgets more efficiently by targeting those channels that deliver the best results. In addition, digital marketing allows businesses to customize and optimize their marketing campaigns in real-time, resulting in further cost savings.

INTERACTION AND CUSTOMER LOYALTY

Digital marketing offers businesses the opportunity to interact directly with their customers and build long-term customer loyalty. By leveraging social media, email marketing, and other digital channels, businesses can engage with their customers, receive feedback, and respond to questions or concerns. These interactions build trust and strengthen the relationship between the company and the customer. By providing relevant and useful content, companies can retain their customers in the long term and turn them into brand ambassadors.

COMPETITIVE ADVANTAGE

Digital marketing offers businesses the opportunity to differentiate themselves from their competitors and gain a competitive advantage. Businesses that use digital marketing effectively can increase brand awareness, attract new customers, and increase sales. By leveraging innovative digital marketing strategies, businesses can better reach their target audience and communicate their marketing messages more effectively. This allows them to differentiate themselves and thrive in an increasingly competitive market.

Overall, digital marketing is now essential for businesses that want to be successful. It offers numerous benefits and opportunities that traditional marketing methods can't provide. By leveraging different digital channels, businesses can effectively reach their target audience, create personalized content, measure the success of their marketing campaigns, and save costs. In addition, digital marketing allows businesses to interact directly with their customers and build long-term customer loyalty. Businesses that use digital marketing effectively can gain a competitive advantage and succeed.

THE EVOLUTION OF DIGITAL MARKETING

Digital marketing has evolved a lot over the years and has become an integral part of companies' marketing strategies. In this section, we'll look at the evolution of digital marketing and provide an overview of its key milestones.

THE BEGINNINGS OF DIGITAL MARKETING

The beginnings of digital marketing date back to the 1990s, when the internet was becoming more and more important. Companies began to establish their presence online and create websites to showcase their products and services. However, at the time, the possibilities of digital marketing were still limited.

THE ERA OF SEARCH ENGINES

With the advent of search engines such as Yahoo and later Google, new opportunities for digital marketing opened up. Businesses realized that they could optimize their websites for search engines to be more easily found in search results. Search engine optimization (SEO) has become an important discipline in digital marketing.

THE ERA OF SOCIAL MEDIA

With the rise of platforms like Facebook, Twitter, and Instagram, a new era of digital marketing began. Companies recognized the potential of social media to connect with their target audience and increase their brand awareness. Social media marketing has become an important tool for reaching and retaining customers.

THE ERA OF MOBILE MARKETING

With the advent of smartphones and tablets, digital marketing has evolved once again. Businesses have had to adapt their marketing strategies to reach mobile users. Mobile marketing and app marketing have become important areas of digital marketing as more and more people use their mobile devices to access the internet.

THE ERA OF DATA-DRIVEN MARKETING

With the increasing availability of data and analytics tools, digital marketing has evolved. Businesses can now gather detailed information about their target audience and optimize their marketing strategies based on this data. Data-driven marketing allows businesses to create personalized content and tailored advertising campaigns.

THE FUTURE OF DIGITAL MARKETING

Digital marketing is an ever-evolving field, and the future promises even more exciting developments. Artificial intelligence, virtual reality, and the Internet of Things are expected to play an increasingly important role in digital marketing. Companies must continuously adapt to new technologies and trends in order to remain competitive.

In this section, we have provided an overview of the evolution of digital marketing. From the early days of the internet to the current trends and developments, digital marketing has become an indispensable tool for businesses. In the following sections, we will look at the basics of digital marketing and the different marketing strategies in detail.

THE BENEFITS OF DIGITAL MARKETING

Digital marketing offers a variety of benefits for businesses and marketers. In this section, we'll take a closer look at the key benefits of digital marketing.

GREATER REACH AND TARGET GROUP TARGETING

A major advantage of digital marketing is the ability to reach a much larger audience than traditional marketing methods. Through the internet and the various digital channels, companies can send their messages to people all over the world. Whether it's a local, national, or international audience, digital marketing allows businesses to expand their reach and target potential customers effectively.

COST SAVINGS

Compared to traditional marketing methods such as print advertising or television commercials, digital marketing tends to be more cost-effective. Digital advertising campaigns can be customized to suit a company's unique needs and budget. There are a variety of low-cost digital marketing channels such as social media, email marketing, and search engine marketing that help businesses achieve their marketing goals without having to spend a fortune.

MEASURABILITY AND ANALYSIS

Another great benefit of digital marketing is the ability to accurately measure and analyze the success of a marketing campaign. Tools like Google Analytics allow businesses to track key metrics like website traffic, conversion rates, and clicks. This data allows companies to continuously optimize their marketing strategies and maximize their returns. Unlike traditional marketing methods, where it is difficult to accurately measure the success of a campaign, digital marketing offers a high level of transparency and accuracy in measuring success.

PERSONALIZATION AND TARGETING

Digital marketing allows companies to tailor their marketing messages to individual audiences. By analyzing data such as demographic information, interests, and behaviors, businesses can create personalized content and advertising tailored to the specific needs and interests of their target audience. These personalized approaches lead to greater relevance and effectiveness of marketing campaigns and increase the chances of a positive response from the target audience.

INTERACTION AND ENGAGEMENT

Digital marketing offers businesses the opportunity to interact directly with their target audience and generate a high level of engagement. Through social media, email marketing, and other digital channels, businesses can communicate with their customers in real-time, receive feedback, and respond to questions or concerns. These interactions strengthen the relationship between business and customers and foster customer trust and loyalty.

FLEXIBILITY AND ADAPTABILITY

Unlike traditional marketing methods, digital marketing offers a high degree of flexibility and adaptability. Businesses can quickly adjust and optimize their marketing strategies and campaigns based on current market conditions and the needs of their target audience. By using real-time data and analytics, businesses can continuously improve their marketing efforts and stay up-to-date.

GLOBAL PRESENCE AND 24/7 AVAILABILITY

Digital marketing allows businesses to have a round-the-clock presence and offer their products or services worldwide. By having a well-designed website and effective search engine optimization, businesses can increase their visibility in search engine results and reach potential customers all over the world. In addition, by using e-commerce solutions, businesses can sell their products or services online and thus generate sales around the clock.

These were some of the key benefits of digital marketing. In the following chapters, we'll take a closer look at the different aspects of digital marketing and how you can take advantage of these benefits to successfully achieve your marketing goals.

THE BASICS OF DIGITAL MARKETING

TARGET GROUP ANALYSIS

Audience analysis is a crucial step in digital marketing. Before you can develop a marketing strategy and choose channels, you need to know your target audience intimately. A thorough audience analysis allows you to target your marketing activities to the needs and interests of your potential customers.

WHY IS AUDIENCE ANALYSIS IMPORTANT?

Audience analysis is of great importance because it helps you use your marketing resources effectively. By defining your target audience, you can ensure that your messages and offers resonate with the right people. This will increase the likelihood that potential customers will respond to your marketing efforts and ultimately become paying customers.

Accurate audience analysis also allows you to tailor your marketing messages and channels in the best possible way. You can tailor the language, tone, and visual design of your content to appeal to the needs and preferences of your target audience. In addition, you can choose the right channels to effectively reach your target audience. This saves time, money, and resources by allowing you to focus on the channels that are most likely to reach your target audience.

HOW DO YOU CONDUCT AN AUDIENCE ANALYSIS?

To conduct an audience analysis, there are several steps you can follow:

1. Market research: Start by thoroughly analyzing the market and industry you're in. Examine current trends, competitors, and customer needs. This will give you an overview of the market and help you better understand your target audience.
2. Demographics: Identify the demographics of your target audience, such as age, gender, income, education level, and geographic location. This information will help you define your target audience more precisely and tailor your marketing messages accordingly.
3. Psychographics: Go beyond demographics and analyze the psychographics of your target audience. This includes their values, interests, lifestyles, and attitudes. By understanding these characteristics, you can better tailor your marketing messages and offers to the needs and preferences of your target audience.
4. Behavioral patterns: Examine the behavior of your target audience, both online and offline. What websites do they visit? What social media do they use? What products do they buy? By understanding the behavior of your target audience, you can choose the right channels and adjust your marketing strategy accordingly.
5. Customer surveys and feedback: Conduct customer surveys and collect feedback from your target audience. This gives you direct insights into their needs, wants, and challenges. You can use this information to further optimize your marketing messages and offers.

THE IMPORTANCE OF CONTINUOUS AUDIENCE ANALYSIS

Audience analysis is not a one-time process. Your audience's needs and preferences can change over time, as can the market and competitors. Therefore, it is important to regularly update and adapt the target group analysis.

Through continuous audience analysis, you can ensure that your marketing strategy is always up-to-date and continues to reach your target audience effectively. You can identify new trends and behavioral patterns and adjust your marketing messages accordingly. This will allow you to stay competitive and achieve your marketing goals.

Audience analysis is an indispensable step in digital marketing. By knowing your target audience intimately, you can target your marketing efforts and increase the likelihood that potential customers will respond to your messages. Conduct a thorough audience analysis and update it regularly to ensure that your marketing strategy is always up to date.

THE MARKETING STRATEGY

Marketing strategy is a crucial part of digital marketing. It establishes the framework within which all marketing activities are carried out. A well-thought-out and effective marketing strategy is the key to success in the digital age. In this section, we'll take a closer look at the different aspects of marketing strategy and show you how to create a strategy that fits your business.

OBJECTIVE

Before you start developing your marketing strategy, it's important to define clear goals. What do you want to achieve with your digital marketing? Do you want to increase your awareness, generate more leads, or increase sales? By setting clear goals, you can target your marketing efforts and measure success.

TARGET GROUP ANALYSIS

To develop an effective marketing strategy, you need to know your target audience intimately. Who are your potential customers? What are their needs, desires and challenges? Through a thorough audience analysis, you can tailor your marketing messages and activities to the needs of your target audience, thus building stronger loyalty.

COMPETITOR ANALYSIS

A competitive analysis is an important step in developing your marketing strategy. You should analyze your direct competitors and understand how they are doing their digital marketing. What channels do they use? What messages do they communicate? By analyzing your competitors, you can learn from their successes and mistakes and adjust your own strategy accordingly.

POSITIONING

Positioning is another important aspect of your marketing strategy. How do you want to be perceived by your target group? What makes your company unique and different from your competitors? By clearly defining your positioning, you can target your marketing messages and build a strong brand.

MARKETING CHANNELS

Choosing the right marketing channels is critical to the success of your marketing strategy. There are a variety of channels you can use, such as search engine marketing, social media marketing, email marketing, and content marketing. It's important to choose the channels that best suit your target audience and goals. A thorough analysis of the different channels and their advantages and disadvantages is therefore essential.

BUDGETING

Budgeting is an important part of your marketing strategy. How much money are you willing to spend on your digital marketing? By setting a budget, you can better plan and manage your marketing activities. It's important to plan the budget carefully and make sure it's enough to meet your goals.

IMPLEMENTATION AND MONITORING

Once you've developed your marketing strategy, it's important to implement it consistently and review it regularly. Monitor the performance of your marketing efforts and adjust your strategy as needed. The digital world is constantly changing, so it's important to be flexible and adapt to new trends and developments.

MEASURING SUCCESS

Measuring success is a crucial step in evaluating the success of your marketing strategy. Define clear metrics and regularly measure how well your marketing efforts are performing. Analyze the data and draw conclusions to continuously improve and optimize your strategy.

A well-thought-out marketing strategy is the key to success in digital marketing. By carefully planning and executing your goals, target audience, competitors, positioning, marketing channels, budgeting, implementation and control, as well as performance measurement, you can target your marketing activities to the needs of your target group and increase success.

In the next few sections, we will take a closer look at the different aspects of digital marketing, such as search engine optimization, search engine marketing, social media marketing, content marketing, email marketing, and mobile marketing.

CHOOSING THE RIGHT CHANNELS

Choosing the right channels is a crucial step in implementing a successful digital marketing strategy. There are a variety of channels that businesses can use to reach their target audience and spread their message. In this section, we'll take a closer look at the different channels and help you choose the right ones for your business.

THE IMPORTANCE OF CHANNEL SELECTION

Choosing the right channels is of great importance as it has a direct impact on the success of your marketing campaigns. Each channel has its own advantages and disadvantages and reaches different audiences. By choosing the right channels, you can ensure that your message is communicated effectively and reaches your target audience.

TARGET GROUP ANALYSIS

Before choosing the channels, you need to analyze your target audience carefully. Who are your potential customers? Where do they hang out online? Which channels do they use the most? By answering these questions, you can better understand your target audience and identify the channels that suit them best.

One way to get to know your target audience better is to conduct surveys or analyze customer data. You can also use social media to gain insights into your target audience's behavior and preferences. The better you understand your target audience, the more targeted you can plan your marketing activities.

THE DIFFERENT CHANNELS

There are a variety of channels you can use for your digital marketing. Here are some of the most popular ones:

Search Engine Marketing (SEM)

Search engine marketing involves placing ads on search engines such as Google or Bing. These ads are shown based on users' search terms and can be an effective way to reach your target audience. Search engine marketing offers a high reach and allows you to tailor your ads precisely to your target audience.

Social Media Marketing

Social media marketing involves using platforms such as Facebook, Instagram, Twitter, and LinkedIn to reach your target audience. These channels offer the opportunity to spread your message to a wide audience and connect with your customers. Social media marketing also allows you to accurately segment your target audience and run targeted ads.

E-Mail-Marketing

Email marketing is an effective way to stay in touch with your customers and let them know about news, offers, and events. By building an email list, you can communicate with your customers on a regular basis and keep them loyal to your business. Email marketing also provides an opportunity to send personalized messages and measure the success of your campaigns.

Content Marketing

Content marketing involves creating and distributing high-quality content to engage and engage your target audience. This can be in the form of blog posts, videos, infographics, or ebooks. By providing valuable content, you can gain the trust of your target audience and get them to interact with your business.

CHOOSING THE RIGHT CHANNELS

To choose the right channels for your business, you should follow the steps below:

1. Analyze your target audience: Understand who your potential customers are and where they hang out online.
2. Define your goals: Determine what you want to achieve with your digital marketing strategy. Do you want to generate more traffic to your website, generate leads, or increase sales?
3. Consider your budget: Consider how much you can spend on your digital marketing and which channels are within that budget.
4. Evaluate the channels: Examine the different channels and evaluate which ones best fit your goals and target audience. Also, consider the pros and cons of each channel.
5. Test and optimize: Once you've selected your channels, it's important to review and optimize them regularly. Analyze the results of your marketing activities and adjust your strategy accordingly.

By following these steps, you can ensure that you choose the right channels for your digital marketing and achieve your marketing goals effectively.

RESULT

Choosing the right channels is a crucial step in implementing a successful digital marketing strategy. By analyzing your target audience, defining your goals, and evaluating the different channels, you can ensure that you choose the right channels to effectively communicate your message and reach your target audience. Keep in mind that channel selection is an ongoing process and requires regular review and optimization.

MEASURING SUCCESS IN DIGITAL MARKETING

Measuring success in digital marketing is a crucial step in evaluating and optimizing the success of your marketing activities. By using the right metrics and tools, you can measure the ROI (return on investment) of your digital marketing campaigns and gain valuable insights to improve your future strategies.

THE IMPORTANCE OF MEASURING SUCCESS

Measuring success in digital marketing is of great importance because it allows you to objectively evaluate the success of your marketing efforts. Without effective performance measurement, you can't accurately determine which marketing activities are working and which aren't. By measuring and analyzing your results, you can make informed decisions and use your resources more efficiently.

CHOOSING THE RIGHT METRICS

When measuring success in digital marketing, there are a variety of metrics you can consider. It's important to choose the ones that best fit your goals and marketing strategy. Here are some of the most important metrics to consider:

- Conversion rate: The conversion rate measures the percentage of visitors who take a desired action on your website, such as making a purchase or signing up for your newsletter. A high conversion rate indicates that your marketing efforts are successful.
- Click-through rate (CTR): The click-through rate measures the percentage of people who clicked on a link or ad. A high CTR indicates that your ads or links are engaging and grabbing users' attention.

- Cost per click (CPC): Cost per click is how much you pay per click on your ads or links. A low CPC indicates that you're running your ads efficiently and saving costs.
- Return on Investment (ROI): ROI measures the ratio between the cost of your marketing efforts and the profit generated. A positive ROI indicates that your marketing efforts are profitable.
- Engagement rate: The engagement rate measures how users interact with your content, such as likes, comments, or shares on social media platforms. A high engagement rate indicates that your content is relevant and engaging.
- Bounce rate: Bounce rate measures the percentage of users who leave your site after visiting a page without taking any further action. A low bounce rate indicates that your website is user-friendly and encourages users to linger.

USE THE RIGHT TOOLS

To effectively measure success in digital marketing, it's important to use the right tools. There are a variety of tools that can help you track and analyze your marketing metrics. Here are some of the most popular tools:

- Google Analytics: Google Analytics is a free tool from Google that gives you detailed insights into how users are behaving on your website. You can use it to track metrics such as visitor numbers, conversion rates, and bounce rates.
- Social media analytics tools: Platforms like Facebook, Twitter, and Instagram offer their own analytics tools to help you measure the performance of your social media posts. You can use it to track metrics such as engagement rates, reach, and impressions.
- Email marketing tools: Email marketing tools like Mailchimp or Sendinblue offer features to measure the success of your email campaigns. You can use it to track metrics such as open rate, click-through rate, and unsubscribe rate.

- A/B testing tools: A/B testing tools like Optimizely or Google Optimize allow you to test different versions of your website or ads to see which ones work better. You can use it to compare metrics such as conversion rates and click-through rates.

CONTINUOUS OPTIMISATION

Measuring success in digital marketing is a continuous process. It's not enough to just analyze your metrics once. You should regularly review your results and optimize your marketing strategy accordingly. Here are some tips on how to continuously improve your performance measurement:

- Set clear goals: Define clear goals for your marketing efforts and determine what metrics you want to use to evaluate those goals.
- Compare yourself to the competition: Regularly analyze the performance of your competitors and draw conclusions for your own marketing strategy.
- Test different approaches: Run A/B tests to test different approaches and see which ones work best.
- Stay up-to-date: Learn about the latest trends and developments in digital marketing and adjust your strategy accordingly.
- Learn from your mistakes: Analyze your failures as well and learn from them. Identify the reasons for failure and optimize your strategy accordingly.

Measuring success in digital marketing is an indispensable part of your marketing strategy. By using the right metrics and tools and continuously optimizing them, you can increase the success of your marketing efforts and achieve your goals more effectively.

SEARCH ENGINE OPTIMIZATION (SEO)

BASICS OF SEARCH ENGINE OPTIMIZATION

Search engine optimization (SEO) is one of the most important disciplines in digital marketing. It includes all measures that serve to place a website as high as possible in the organic search results of search engines such as Google, Bing or Yahoo. By ranking well in search results, businesses can increase their visibility on the internet and drive more potential customers to their website.

WHY IS SEARCH ENGINE OPTIMIZATION IMPORTANT?

The importance of search engine optimization lies in the fact that most internet users use search engines to search for information, products, or services. Studies have shown that the majority of clicks are on the first pages of results, while the sites placed further down receive less attention. Therefore, it is of great importance for companies to appear as high as possible in the search results in order to increase the chance of clicks and visitors.

HOW DOES SEARCH ENGINE OPTIMIZATION WORK?

Search engine optimization is based on various factors that are taken into account by search engine algorithms. These algorithms evaluate websites based on criteria such as relevance, quality, and user experience. In order to optimize a website for search engines, several aspects must be taken into account:

Keyword Research & Optimization

Keyword research is an important first step in search engine optimization. It identifies relevant search terms that potential customers use to search for specific products or services. These keywords should then be strategically placed in the website's content to increase relevance to search engines.

On-Page Optimization

On-page optimization refers to all actions that are carried out directly on the website to improve search engine optimization. This includes optimizing meta tags, headings, URLs, images, and internal links. By optimizing these elements, search engines can better understand and index the site's content.

Off-Page Optimization

Off-page optimization refers to actions taken outside the website that serve to increase the visibility and authority of the website. This includes, for example, building backlinks, i.e. linking from other websites to your own website, as well as participating in relevant business directories and social media platforms. Building high-quality backlinks can increase the authority of the website, which has a positive effect on ranking in search results.

Technical SEO Optimization

Technical SEO optimization refers to all the technical aspects of a website that can affect search engine optimization. These include, for example, the loading time of the website, mobile optimization, the XML sitemap and the robots.txt file. A technically sound website is easier for search engines to index and understand, which can have a positive impact on ranking.

SEO TOOLS & TRENDS

To carry out search engine optimization effectively, there are various tools available to help businesses analyze and optimize their website. These include, for example, Google Analytics, Google Search Console, Moz, SEMrush, and Ahrefs. These tools offer features such as keyword research, competitor analysis, backlink analysis, and ranking monitoring.

In addition, there are also various trends and developments in the field of search engine optimization that businesses should keep an eye on. These include, for example, the increasing importance of voice search, the increasing relevance of local search engine optimization and the integration of artificial intelligence into search engine algorithms.

Search engine optimization is a complex topic that requires continuous work and adjustments. However, by implementing the fundamentals of search engine optimization, businesses can improve their visibility in search results and drive more potential customers to their website.

KEYWORD RESEARCH & OPTIMIZATION

Keyword research and optimization is a crucial step in search engine optimization (SEO). By choosing the right keywords, you can ensure that your website appears in search results when potential customers search for relevant information or products. In this section, we'll take a closer look at keyword research and optimization, and show you how to optimize your website for specific keywords.

THE IMPORTANCE OF KEYWORD RESEARCH

Keyword research is the process of identifying and selecting the most relevant keywords for your website. It's important to choose keywords that are commonly used by your target audience and have a high search volume. By using these keywords, you can ensure that your website shows up in search results and that potential customers come to your website.

To find the right keywords, you can use various tools and techniques. One way is to use Google's search suggestions. Just type a relevant keyword into the Google search bar and check out the automatic suggestions. These suggestions are based on users' most common searches and can give you valuable insights into the keywords you should use.

Another useful tool for keyword research is Google Keyword Planner. With this tool, you can analyze the search volume and competitiveness of keywords. You can also discover similar keywords that might be relevant to your website. Google Keyword Planner is a free tool that can help you find the right keywords for your website.

KEYWORD OPTIMIZATION

Once you've identified the most relevant keywords for your website, it's important to place those keywords in strategic areas of your website. This is known as keyword optimization, and it helps search engines better understand your website and rank it higher in search results.

An important area where you should place your keywords is your website's title tag. The title tag is the title that appears in search results and should contain the main keyword of your page. Make sure the title tag is concise and engaging to encourage potential visitors to click.

Another important area for keyword optimization is the meta description tag. The meta description is a short description of your page that will also appear in the search results. Use your keywords in the meta description to give users an overview of your page's content and encourage them to click.

In addition, you should also use your keywords in the headings of your page. Use the main keyword in the H1 headline and use related keywords in the H2 and H3 headings. This helps search engines better understand the content of your page and make it more relevant in search results.

It's also important to use your keywords in the body of your page. Place your keywords naturally and organically in the text without exaggerating. Use synonyms and related terms to expand your page's content and show search engines that your page offers comprehensive information on a particular topic.

THE IMPORTANCE OF KEYWORD DENSITY

Keyword density refers to the ratio between the number of keywords on a page and the total number of words on that page. Proper keyword density can help your page rank higher in search results. However, it's important not to overdo keyword density, as it can be considered spamming and can lead to a penalty from search engines.

There is no exact rule for the optimal keyword density, as it depends on various factors, such as the type of content and the competition in your niche. However, as a rule of thumb, your keywords should make up about 1-2% of the total number of words on the page. Make sure that your keywords are placed naturally and organically in the text, and that the content is relevant and useful to readers.

CONTINUOUS MONITORING AND ADJUSTMENT OF YOUR KEYWORDS

Keyword research and optimization is an ongoing process. It's important to regularly monitor and adjust your keywords to ensure they continue to be relevant and effective. Regularly check the search volume and competitiveness of your keywords and adjust your strategy accordingly.

You can also use tools to monitor the ranking of your keywords in search results. These tools will show you how well your website ranks for specific keywords and if there are any changes needed to your keyword strategy. Also, monitor the performance of your competitors and analyze their keyword strategy to gain valuable insights.

Keyword research and optimization is an important step in optimizing your website for search engines and generating more organic traffic. Take the time to find the right keywords for your website and place them strategically. Monitor your keywords regularly and adjust your strategy to make sure your website ranks well in search results.

ON-PAGE OPTIMIZATION

On-page optimization is an important part of search engine optimization (SEO). It refers to all the actions that are carried out on one's own website to improve its visibility in search engine results. By optimizing the content and technical aspects of the website, you can ensure that your page is better recognized and ranked by search engines like Google. In this section, we'll take a closer look at the different aspects of on-page optimization and show you how to optimize your website for search engines.

META TAGS AND TITLE TAGS

Meta tags and title tags are important elements of on-page optimization. They are used to provide search engines with information about the content of your website. The title tag is the title that appears in search engine results, while the meta tags provide a brief description of the content. It's important to use descriptive and relevant title tags and meta tags that grab users' attention and give them an overview of your page's content.

URL STRUCTURE

Your website's URL structure also plays an important role in on-page optimization. A clear and descriptive URL structure makes it easier for search engines to understand and index the content of your page. Use descriptive keywords in your URLs and avoid long and confusing strings. A well-structured URL will also make it easier for users to understand and navigate your website.

HEADINGS AND FORMATTING

Using headings and clear formatting is another important aspect of on-page optimization. Search engines evaluate headings as clues to the content of a page. Therefore, use relevant keywords in your headlines to signal to search engines what your page is about. In addition, you should structure your text well and use paragraphs, lists, and bold text to make the content easy to read and understand.

KEYWORD DENSITY AND KEYWORD OPTIMIZATION

Keyword density refers to the ratio between the number of keywords and the total text on a page. It's important to choose your keywords carefully and use them naturally and organically in your texts. Excessive keyword density can be considered spamming by search engines and cause your page to depreciate. Make sure that your keywords are meaningfully embedded in the text and that the content is relevant and useful to users.

INTERNAL LINKING

Internal linking is another important aspect of on-page optimization. By putting internal links on your website, you can make it easier to navigate and help users find relevant content. Search engines also use internal links to understand the connection between different pages of your website. Make sure your internal links are relevant and well-placed to improve the user experience and increase your page's visibility.

IMAGES AND ALTERNATIVE TEXTS

Images play an important role in designing an engaging website. However, they can also help improve on-page optimization. Use descriptive file names for your images and add alternative text that describes the content of the image. Search engines can read alternative texts and use them as additional information to understand the content of your page. By optimizing your images, you can improve your website's visibility in search engine results.

LOADING TIME OPTIMIZATION

Your website's loading time is another important factor in on-page optimization. Slow loading time can cause users to abandon your page and lead to a higher bounce rate. Search engines also take load time into account when evaluating your page. Therefore, optimize the size of your images, minimize code, and use caching techniques to improve your website's loading time. A fast and responsive website is appreciated by users and rewarded by search engines.

RESULT

On-page optimization is an essential part of search engine optimization. By optimizing your website, you can ensure that it is better recognized and ranked by search engines. By using relevant keywords, creating a clear URL structure, using descriptive headlines, and optimizing your images, you can improve your website's visibility in search engine results. In addition, you should also optimize your website's loading time to ensure a positive user experience. On-page optimization is a continuous process that requires regular review and adjustment to ensure that your website is always up-to-date and meets the requirements of search engines.

OFF-PAGE OPTIMIZATION

Off-page optimization is an important part of search engine optimization (SEO). While on-page optimization deals with the optimization measures on one's own website, off-page optimization deals with all measures outside one's own website that serve to improve the visibility and authority of the website in search engine results.

BACKLINK BUILDING

A central aspect of off-page optimization is backlink building. Backlinks are links from other websites that point to your own website. Search engines like Google view backlinks as recommendations and rate sites with a lot of high-quality backlinks as more trustworthy and relevant. Therefore, it is important to build high-quality backlinks from topic-relevant and authoritative websites.

There are several strategies to build backlinks. One way is to contact other website operators and offer guest posts or cooperations. You should make sure that the linking websites fit thematically with your own website and have a good reputation. In addition, directory listings, press releases, or sharing content on social media can also help generate backlinks.

SOCIAL SIGNALS

Another important aspect of off-page optimization is so-called social signals. These are signals that come from social media such as Facebook, Twitter or Instagram and indicate the relevance and popularity of a website. Search engines take these signals into account when evaluating websites.

To generate social signals, it is important to create high-quality and relevant content that will be shared and liked by users on social media. In addition, interacting with users on social media can help to increase the visibility and reach of your website.

ONLINE REPUTATION MANAGEMENT

Another aspect of off-page optimization is online reputation management. The aim is to monitor the reputation of one's own brand or website on the Internet and, if necessary, to improve it. A positive online reputation is important to gain user trust and increase visibility in search engine results.

To improve online reputation, it is important to collect and present positive reviews and recommendations from customers. In addition, negative reviews and comments should be actively addressed and resolved to protect the reputation of the brand or website.

INFLUENCER-MARKETING

Influencer marketing is an effective method of off-page optimization to increase the reach and visibility of one's website.

You work with influencers who have a large number of followers on social media and can therefore achieve a high reach.

It is important to choose influencers who fit thematically with your website and appeal to a similar target group. By collaborating with influencers, high-quality content can be created and disseminated that will be noticed and shared by the influencer's followers.

MONITORING AND ANALYSIS

In order to measure and improve the success of off-page optimization, it is important to regularly monitor and analyze the measures taken. Various key figures such as the number of backlinks, the number of social shares or the development of online reputation should be monitored.

By analysing the data, weaknesses can be identified and optimisation potentials uncovered. Based on these findings, targeted measures can then be taken to further improve off-page optimization and increase the visibility of your own website in search engine results.

Off-page optimization is an important part of digital marketing and goes a long way in improving a website's visibility and authority. Off-page optimization can be successfully implemented through the targeted development of backlinks, the generation of social signals, the management of online reputation, influencer marketing and the regular analysis of the measures carried out.

TECHNICAL SEO OPTIMIZATION

Technical SEO optimization is a crucial factor in your website's success in search engine results. It's all about making sure that your website is technically sound and can be easily searched and indexed by search engines. In this section, we'll look at the most important aspects of technical SEO optimization and show you how to optimize your website for search engines.

OPTIMIZE WEBSITE SPEED

The speed of your website is a crucial factor in ranking in search engine results. A slow website can scare off visitors and lead to a higher bounce rate. In addition, search engines prefer fast websites as they provide a better user experience. There are several ways to optimize the speed of your website:

- Compress images: Images are often the largest files on a website. By compressing the images, you can significantly reduce the loading time of your website without sacrificing the quality of the images.
- Minimize code: By removing unnecessary code and minimizing CSS and JavaScript files, you can reduce your website's load time.
- Use caching: Caching allows you to further optimize your website's load time by caching static content and retrieving it when needed.
- Optimize your server configuration: Poor server configuration can lead to a slow website. Make sure your server is properly configured and has sufficient resources to handle traffic to your website.

MOBILE OPTIMIZATION

With the increasing use of mobile devices, it is imperative to optimize your website for mobile users. Search engines prefer mobile-optimized websites and reward them with a better ranking in search results. Here are some important aspects of mobile optimization:

- Responsive design: Make sure your website has a responsive design that automatically adapts to different screen sizes.
- Mobile Usability: Optimize your website's usability for mobile users by using large buttons, easy-to-read text, and easy navigation.
- Mobile load time: Make sure your website loads quickly on mobile devices to ensure a positive user experience.

- Mobile crawling: Make sure search engines can easily crawl and index your mobile site.

OPTIMIZE URL STRUCTURE

Optimizing your website's URL structure can help search engines better understand and index your content. Here are some best practices for optimizing your URL structure:

- Use descriptive URLs: Use clear and descriptive URLs that reflect the content of the page. Avoid long and confusing URLs with lots of special characters.
- Use hyphens instead of underscores: Use hyphens to separate words in your URL instead of using underscores. Search engines prefer hyphens because they are better at recognizing words.
- Avoid dynamic URLs: Avoid dynamic URLs with lots of parameters and numbers. Make sure your URLs are static and user-friendly.

CREATE A SITEMAP

A sitemap is an XML file that lists all the pages of your website and helps search engines crawl and index your website efficiently. By creating a sitemap, you can ensure that all pages of your website are captured by search engines. Here are some tips for creating a sitemap:

- Use an XML sitemap: XML is the preferred format for sitemaps. Make sure your sitemap is in XML format.
- Update your sitemap regularly: If you're adding new pages or updating existing pages, be sure to update your sitemap accordingly.
- Check your sitemap for errors: Make sure that there are no errors in your sitemap and that all URLs are listed correctly.

USING CANONICAL TAGS

Canonical tags are HTML tags that tell search engines which version of a page should be considered the preferred version when multiple versions of the same page are available. By using canonical tags, you can ensure that search engines index and display the right content. Here are some tips for using canonical tags:

- Use canonical tags for duplicate content: If you have multiple versions of the same page, such as a desktop version and a mobile version, you should use canonical tags to tell search engines which version to prefer.
- Check your canonical tags regularly: Make sure your canonical tags are implemented correctly and point to the correct version of the page.

SEO TOOLS & TRENDS

Search engine optimization (SEO) is an essential part of digital marketing. To optimize your website for search engines and rank better in search results, it's important to know the right SEO tools and trends. In this section, we'll share some of the most popular SEO tools and discuss current trends to consider in your SEO strategy.

KEYWORD-SEARCH-TOOLS

Keyword research is an important step in optimizing your website for search engines. With the right keywords, you can ensure that your content is found by the right audiences. There are several tools that can help you with keyword research. A popular tool is Google Keyword Planner. With this tool, you can find relevant keywords for your website and get information such as the average monthly search volume and competition for each keyword. Other popular keyword research tools include SEMrush, Ahrefs, and Moz Keyword Explorer.

ON-PAGE OPTIMIZATION TOOLS

On-page optimization refers to optimizing the content and structure of your website to make it attractive to search engines and users alike. There are several tools that can help you with on-page optimization. A popular tool is Yoast SEO. This WordPress plugin provides comprehensive on-page analysis and gives you recommendations on how to optimize your content. Another useful tool is Screaming Frog SEO Spider. With this tool, you can crawl your website and identify technical issues such as missing meta tags, broken links, and slow loading times.

BACKLINK-ANALYSE-TOOLS

Backlinks play an important role in SEO because they can increase your website's trust and authority. There are several tools that can help you analyze your backlinks. A popular tool is Ahrefs. With Ahrefs, you can monitor your website's backlinks, analyze your competitors' backlinks, and find potential link building opportunities. Another useful tool is Moz Link Explorer. This tool provides detailed information about your website's backlinks, including the Domain Authority and Spam Score of the referring domains.

RANK-TRACKING-TOOLS

Tracking your website's ranking in search results is crucial to measuring the success of your SEO strategy. There are several tools that can help you monitor your website's ranking. A popular tool is SEMrush. With SEMrush, you can track your website's ranking for specific keywords and analyze your competitors' rankings. Another useful tool is Google Search Console. With this free tool from Google, you can monitor your website's ranking, identify technical issues, and gain insights into your website's performance in search results.

VOICE SEARCH & MOBILE OPTIMIZATION

A current trend in the field of search engine optimization is voice search. More and more people are using voice assistants such as Siri, Google Assistant, and Amazon Alexa to search for information. Therefore, it is important to optimize your website for voice search. Make sure your content is written in natural language and responds to users' questions and needs. In addition, mobile optimization of your website is another important trend. With more and more people accessing the internet via mobile devices, it's important that your website is optimized for mobile devices. Make sure your website loads quickly, is user-friendly, and has a responsive design.

LOCAL SEO AND GOOGLE MY BUSINESS

For companies with a local focus, local search engine optimization is of great importance. Local SEO refers to optimizing your website to be found better in local search results. An important aspect of local SEO is setting up and optimizing a Google My Business listing. Google My Business allows you to provide information such as your opening hours, address, phone number, and collect customer reviews. Make sure your Google My Business listing is complete and up-to-date to increase your chances of ranking well in local search results.

TECHNICAL SEO TOOLS

Technical search engine optimization refers to optimizing the technical aspects of your website to ensure that it can be properly indexed and interpreted by search engines. There are several tools that can help you with technical SEO. A popular tool is Google Search Console. Google Search Console can help you identify and fix technical issues such as crawl errors, missing meta tags, and slow load times. Another useful tool is Screaming Frog SEO Spider. With this tool, you can crawl your website and identify technical issues such as missing meta tags, broken links, and slow loading times.

SUMMARY

In this section, we've shared some of the most important SEO tools and trends. Using these tools can help you optimize your website for search engines and rank better in search results. In addition, it is important to consider the current trends in search engine optimization, such as voice search, mobile optimization, and local SEO. By incorporating these tools and trends into your SEO strategy, you can further increase the success of your digital marketing.

SEARCH ENGINE MARKETING (SEM)

BASICS OF SEARCH ENGINE MARKETING

Search engine marketing (SEM) is an important part of digital marketing. It encompasses all the measures taken to improve a website's visibility in search engine results. SEM consists of two main components: search engine optimization (SEO) and paid search advertising.

THE IMPORTANCE OF SEARCH ENGINE MARKETING

In today's digital world, the internet is the first port of call for many people looking for information, products, or services. Search engines like Google are the most used platforms to answer these search queries. Therefore, it is crucial for businesses to have a presence in search engine results to reach potential customers.

Search engine marketing offers companies the opportunity to increase their visibility in search engine results and to address relevant target groups in a targeted manner. By combining SEO and paid search advertising, businesses can strengthen their online presence and effectively achieve their marketing goals.

GOOGLE ADS AND OTHER AD NETWORKS

Google Ads is the most well-known and widely used advertising network for search engine marketing. It allows businesses to place ads in Google's search engine results and target for relevant keywords. Google Ads offers different advertising formats such as text ads, display ads, and video ads to meet the different needs of businesses.

In addition to Google Ads, there are other ad networks that businesses can use to expand their search engine marketing strategy. For example, Bing Ads is Microsoft's ad network and offers similar features to Google Ads. It's a good alternative to get extra reach and reach potential customers who use Bing as their search engine.

KEYWORD-ADVERTISING

Keyword advertising is one of the most effective strategies in search engine marketing. It refers to serving ads based on specific keywords typed into search engines by the users. By choosing relevant keywords, businesses can ensure that their ads are only shown to those users who are actively searching for their products or services.

Choosing the right keywords is crucial for the success of keyword advertising. It's important to identify keywords that have a high search volume while also matching the company's target audience and offerings. Keyword research tools like Google Keyword Planner can help businesses find the best keywords for their ad campaigns.

DISPLAY ADVERTISING

Display advertising is another important component of search engine marketing. Unlike text ads in search engine results, display ads appear on websites and apps. These ads can appear in the form of banners, images, or videos, and are a way for businesses to increase their brand awareness and engage potential customers in a visual way.

Display ads are typically placed through ad networks such as the Google Display Network. This network includes a variety of websites and apps where businesses can place their ads. By targeting specific audiences and using visually appealing ad formats, businesses can effectively communicate their message and engage potential customers.

REMARKETING UND RETARGETING

Remarketing and retargeting are strategies in search engine marketing that aim to retarget potential customers who have already shown interest in a company's offerings. These strategies are based on the use of cookies to record users' behavior and show them targeted ads based on their previous interactions with the website or products.

Remarketing and retargeting allow businesses to strengthen their brand presence and improve conversion rates by retargeting potential customers and encouraging them to return and take an action, such as making a purchase or signing up for a newsletter.

These strategies can be implemented through various channels, including search advertising, display advertising, and social media. By combining remarketing and retargeting, businesses can target their marketing messages to relevant audiences and effectively achieve their marketing goals.

In this section, we've covered the basics of search engine marketing, including the importance of SEM, the use of Google Ads and other ad networks, keyword advertising strategy, display advertising, and remarketing and retargeting strategies. These fundamentals are crucial to developing a successful search engine marketing strategy and improving a company's visibility and reach in search engine results. In the following sections, we'll delve into more aspects of digital marketing to provide you with a comprehensive understanding and practical tips for your digital marketing success.

GOOGLE ADS AND OTHER AD NETWORKS

Google Ads is one of the most well-known and effective digital marketing platforms. It allows businesses to place ads in Google's search results and target their target audience. However, in addition to Google Ads, there are other ad networks that are worth considering. In this section, we'll take a closer look at Google Ads and other ad networks and how they can be integrated into your marketing strategy.

GOOGLE ADS: AN INTRODUCTION

Google Ads, formerly known as Google AdWords, is an advertising network that allows businesses to place ads on Google's search results pages. It is based on the pay-per-click (PPC) model, where businesses only pay when a user clicks on their ad. Google Ads offers a variety of display formats, including text ads, display ads, video ads, and app ads. It also allows targeting based on keywords, locations, demographics, and interests.

THE BENEFITS OF GOOGLE ADS

Google Ads offers a variety of benefits for businesses that engage in digital marketing. Here are some of the key benefits:

1. Reach: Google is the most used search engine in the world, which means that your ads have a wide reach and can potentially reach many users.
2. Targeted targeting: Google Ads allows you to target your ads to your target audience. You can choose keywords that are relevant to your business and show your ads only to people who search for those keywords.
3. Flexible budget: Google Ads allows you to adjust your budget flexibly. You can choose how much you want to

spend per day or per click, and you have full control over your spending.

4. Measurability: Google Ads allows you to accurately measure the success of your ads. You'll get detailed reports on the number of clicks, impressions, conversion rates, and more. This will allow you to optimize your campaigns and improve your marketing strategy.

OTHER AD NETWORKS

In addition to Google Ads, there are other ad networks that are worth considering. Here are some of the most popular ones:

1. Bing Ads: Bing Ads is Microsoft's ad network and allows businesses to show ads in Bing's search results. Although Bing is not as widely used as Google, it still has a sizable user base and can be a good complement to Google Ads.
2. Social media ad networks: Platforms such as Facebook, Instagram, Twitter, and LinkedIn offer advertising opportunities for businesses. These ad networks allow you to target your ads to specific audiences and offer a variety of display formats, including image ads, video ads, and carousel ads.
3. Display ad networks: Display networks, such as the Google Display Network, allow businesses to serve ads on third-party websites. These ads can be displayed in the form of banners, text ads, or rich media ads and offer wide reach and visibility.
4. Native Advertising Networks: Native advertising networks like Taboola and Outbrain allow businesses to place their content on relevant websites. These types of ad networks seamlessly integrate ads into editorial content and provide a higher chance of users interacting with the ads.

CHOOSING THE RIGHT AD NETWORK

Choosing the right ad network depends on several factors, including your target audience, budget, and marketing goals. It's important to understand your target audience and which platforms they're on the most. For example, if your target audience is primarily active on Facebook, it may make sense to invest in social media ad networks. On the other hand, if you want to target a wider audience, Google Ads can be a good choice.

It's also important to consider your budget. Some ad networks can be more expensive than others, and it's important to make sure you have enough financial resources to run your campaigns effectively.

Finally, you should keep your marketing goals in mind. Do you want to generate more traffic to your website? Do you want to increase your brand awareness? Do you want to get more conversions? Depending on your goals, one particular ad network may be more suitable than others.

Overall, Google Ads and other ad networks offer a variety of ways to achieve your marketing goals. By understanding your target audience, considering your budget, and defining your marketing goals, you can make the right choice and successfully execute your marketing strategy.

KEYWORD-ADVERTISING

Keyword advertising is an effective way to target potential customers and increase your website's visibility in search engine results. This form of search engine marketing involves showing ads that target specific keywords. When a user searches for one of these keywords, your ad will be prominently placed and can thus attract the user's attention.

THE IMPORTANCE OF KEYWORD ADVERTISING

Keyword advertising plays a crucial role in digital marketing because it allows you to reach your target audience when they are actively searching for products or services that you offer. By choosing the right keywords, you can ensure that your ads are only shown to users who have an interest in what you have to offer. This increases the likelihood that these users will click on your ad and visit your website.

In addition, keyword advertising offers a high degree of flexibility and control over your marketing campaigns. You can always customize your ads, add new keywords, or exclude non-relevant keywords. This allows you to continuously optimize your campaigns and get the best results.

THE RIGHT CHOICE OF KEYWORDS

Choosing the right keywords is critical to the success of your keyword advertising campaigns. You should choose relevant keywords that resonate with your offer and target audience. Thorough keyword research is therefore essential.

There are various tools and techniques that can help you with keyword research. One way is to use keyword planning tools like Google Keyword Planner. This tool will show you the search volume and competition for specific keywords, giving you insight into their relevance and potential.

In addition, you can also analyze your competitors and find out what keywords they use in their ads. This can help you come up with new keyword ideas and grow your own keyword list.

DESIGNING EFFECTIVE ADS

To realize the full potential of keyword advertising, it's important to design effective ads. Your ads should be engaging and relevant to grab users' attention and keep them interested.

An important aspect of designing ads is the use of the selected keywords. You'll want to make sure that the keywords in your ad are prominently placed to show users that your ad is relevant to their search query.

In addition, you should also pay attention to the design of the ad text. Use clear and concise language to get your message across effectively. Also, add a clear call-to-action that encourages users to click on your ad and visit your website.

OPTIMIZING YOUR KEYWORD ADVERTISING CAMPAIGNS

Continuously optimizing your keyword advertising campaigns is crucial to get the best results. You should regularly check your keywords and exclude non-relevant keywords. In addition, you can also run A/B tests to compare and improve the performance of your ads.

Another important aspect of optimization is monitoring your campaign performance. You should regularly check click-through rate, conversion rate, and other relevant metrics to see how well your campaigns are performing. Based on this data, you can make adjustments and further optimize your campaigns.

THE COST AND BUDGET OF KEYWORD ADVERTISING

With keyword advertising, you typically pay per click on your ad. The cost per click can vary depending on the competition and the relevance of the keywords. It's important to set a realistic budget and keep an eye on your campaign costs.

One way to control your costs is to use keyword matching. For example, you can choose to show your ads only for certain keywords, or exclude certain keywords to avoid non-relevant clicks.

In addition, you can also use the bidding system to control your ad position. By setting a higher bid, you can rank your ads higher in search results and increase visibility. However, it's important to weigh the costs and benefits to ensure your campaigns remain profitable.

RESULT

Keyword advertising is an effective way to target potential customers and increase your website's visibility in search engine results. By choosing the right keywords, designing engaging ads, and continuously optimizing your campaigns, you can unlock the full potential of keyword advertising and achieve your marketing goals. However, it's important to keep an eye on your costs and regularly monitor and adjust your campaigns for the best results.

DISPLAY ADVERTISING

Display advertising is an effective method of digital marketing to make potential customers aware of your products or services. Display advertising is the act of serving ads on websites, mobile apps, and other digital platforms. These ads can appear in the form of banners, images, videos, or interactive ads.

THE BENEFITS OF DISPLAY ADVERTISING

Display advertising offers a variety of benefits for businesses looking to increase their reach and visibility. Here are some of the key benefits:

1. **Wide reach**: By running ads on different websites and platforms, you can reach a large number of potential customers.
2. **Audience targeting**: Display advertising allows you to fine-tune your audience and target your ads to them. You can take into account demographics, interests, and behaviors to ensure that your ads are shown to the right people.
3. **Visual appeal**: By using engaging visuals such as images and videos, you can grab users' attention and pique their curiosity.
4. **Flexibility**: Display advertising gives you the opportunity to use different ad formats and sizes to present your message in the best possible way. You can also run A/B tests to see which ads work best.
5. **Measurability**: Display advertising allows you to accurately measure the success of your ads. You can track metrics such as clicks, impressions, conversion rates, and cost per conversion to evaluate the effectiveness of your campaigns.

PLANNING A DISPLAY ADVERTISING CAMPAIGN

Before launching a display advertising campaign, it's important to do some thorough planning. Here are some steps to keep in mind:

1. **Objective**: Define clear goals for your campaign. Do you want to increase your brand awareness, increase traffic to your website, or generate direct sales?
2. **Audience Analysis**: Identify your target audience and analyze their demographics, interests, and behaviors. This will help you target your ads.
3. **Budgeting**: Set a budget for your campaign. Consider the cost per click or impression, as well as the total duration of the campaign.

4. **Platform selection**: Choose the appropriate platforms for your ads. Consider the reach, targeting, and cost of the different platforms.
5. **Ad creation**: Create engaging ads that grab users' attention. Use high-quality images or videos and a clear message to persuade your target audience.
6. **Campaign optimization**: Regularly monitor the performance of your ads and optimize them as needed. Test different ad variations to see which ones work best.

CHOOSING THE RIGHT DISPLAY ADVERTISING PLATFORMS

There are a variety of platforms where you can run your display advertising campaigns. Here are some of the most popular platforms:

1. Google Display Network: The Google Display Network offers a wide reach and allows you to place your ads on websites, mobile apps, and YouTube. You can target your ads based on keywords, interests, and demographics.
2. **Social media platforms**: Platforms such as Facebook, Instagram, Twitter, and LinkedIn also offer display advertising opportunities. These platforms allow you to target your ads based on your target audience's demographics, interests, and behaviors.
3. **Programmatic Advertising**: Programmatic advertising allows you to automatically show your ads on different websites and platforms. This method uses algorithms to deliver your ads to the right audience based on real-time data.
4. **Native advertising platforms**: Native advertising platforms such as Taboola and Outbrain offer the ability to place your ads on websites in the form of editorial content. These types of ads blend seamlessly with editorial content and offer higher user adoption.

MEASURING THE SUCCESS OF DISPLAY ADVERTISING CAMPAIGNS

Measuring success is an important part of any display advertising campaign. Here are some metrics to keep in mind:

1. **Impressions**: The number of ad views.
2. Clicks: The number of clicks on your ads.
3. **Conversion rate**: The ratio of clicks to conversions, such as sales or signups.
4. **Cost per click (CPC):** The average price you pay for each click on your ads.
5. **Cost per conversion (CPA):** The average price you pay for each conversion.
6. **View-through** conversions: The number of conversions that occur after the ad is viewed, without a click.

By regularly monitoring and analyzing these metrics, you can evaluate the success of your display advertising campaigns and make adjustments as needed.

RESULT

Display advertising is an effective method of digital marketing to make potential customers aware of your products or services. By targeting and using engaging visuals, you can reach your target audience and measure the success of your campaigns. Choose the appropriate platforms and continuously optimize your ads for maximum results.

REMARKETING UND RETARGETING

Remarketing and retargeting are two important strategies in digital marketing that allow businesses to target potential customers who have already shown interest in their products or services. These strategies are based on the idea that people who have already been exposed to a brand are more inclined to make a purchase decision.

WHAT IS REMARKETING?

Remarketing refers to targeting users who have already visited a website but have not taken a desired action, such as making a purchase or filling out a contact form. Through remarketing, companies can retarget these users and present them with personalized ads to encourage them to return to the site and convert.

The basis of remarketing is a tracking code that is placed on the website and makes it possible to track the activities of visitors. When a user visits the website, a cookie is stored in their browser. This information can then be used to display targeted ads on other websites that the user visits.

HOW DOES REMARKETING WORK?

To use remarketing effectively, it's important to define the target audience and create the right ads. There are different types of remarketing that can be used depending on the target audience and marketing goal:

- **Standard remarketing**: This refers to users who have visited a website but have not converted. They are presented with personalized ads on other websites to encourage them to return.
- **Dynamic** remarketing: This form of remarketing is aimed at users who have viewed certain products or services on the website. They will then be presented with targeted ads with the products they have been interested in. This can increase the incentive to buy and increase the conversion rate.

- **Email remarketing**: This is aimed at users who have left
  their email address on the website but have not converted.
  They will be sent personalized emails with special offers or
  reminders to encourage them to return and complete a
  conversion.

WAS IST RETARGETING?

Retargeting is a similar strategy to remarketing, but with the
difference that it focuses on targeting users who have left a website
without taking a desired action. Retargeting allows businesses to
retarget these users and present them with personalized ads to get
them to return to the site and convert.

Unlike remarketing, retargeting is not based on the visit to a
specific website, but on the user's behavior on the Internet. By
setting cookies, companies can track users' activities and present
them with targeted ads on other websites.

HOW DOES RETARGETING WORK?

Retargeting works similarly to remarketing, but with the difference
that it is based on users' behavior on the internet. There are
different types of retargeting that can be used depending on your
target audience and marketing goal:

- **Site retargeting**: Retargeting users who have visited a
  particular website but have not converted. They are
  presented with personalized ads on other websites to
  encourage them to return.
- **Search** retargeting: This form of retargeting is aimed at
  users who have entered certain search terms into search
  engines but have not converted. They are then presented
  with targeted ads that are tailored to their search queries.
- **Social media retargeting**: This involves retargeting users
  who have visited a website but have not converted. They

will be presented with personalized ads on social media platforms to encourage them to return.

BENEFITS OF REMARKETING AND RETARGETING

Remarketing and retargeting offer a variety of benefits to businesses:

- **Increase conversion rate**: By targeting users who have already shown interest, businesses can increase conversions and generate more sales or leads.
- **Increase** brand awareness: By repeatedly displaying ads, businesses can increase their brand awareness and increase awareness of their products or services.
- **Improve customer retention**: Through personalized ads and emails, businesses can build customer loyalty and build long-term customer relationships.
- **Cost savings**: Because remarketing and retargeting are targeted at potential customers, businesses can optimize their marketing spend and save costs.
- **Measurability and optimization**: Remarketing and retargeting allow businesses to accurately measure and optimize the success of their campaigns. By analyzing data, they can tailor their ads and messaging to get better results.

BEST PRACTICES FÜR REMARKETING UND RETARGETING

For remarketing and retargeting to be successful, it's important to follow a few best practices:

- **Audience** segmentation: Audience segmentation allows businesses to tailor their ads and messages to users' specific needs and interests.
- **Ad personalization**: Personalized ads have a higher chance of success than general ads. Businesses should therefore tailor their ads to users' interests and behavior.

- **Frequency control**: Too high an ad frequency can cause users to be annoyed and have a negative perception of the brand. Businesses should therefore carefully manage ad frequency for optimal impact.
- **A/B** testing: By testing different ad variants, businesses can find out which messages and designs work best and optimize their campaigns accordingly.
- **Optimization of** landing pages: The landing pages should be specifically tailored to the users who are targeted via remarketing and retargeting. They should include clear calls to action and provide value to users.
- **Privacy and transparency**: Companies should ensure that they comply with data protection regulations and communicate transparently with users about how their data is being used.

Remarketing and retargeting are powerful digital marketing strategies that allow businesses to target their target audience and increase conversions. With the right segmentation, personalization, and optimization, businesses can realize the full potential of these strategies and build long-term customer relationships.

SOCIAL MEDIA MARKETING

THE IMPORTANCE OF SOCIAL MEDIA IN MARKETING

Social media has gained enormous importance in the field of marketing in recent years. Platforms like Facebook, Instagram, Twitter, and LinkedIn have become powerful tools to interact with customers, increase brand awareness, and increase sales. In this section, we will take a closer look at the importance of social media in marketing.

THE ROLE OF SOCIAL MEDIA IN MARKETING

Social media has revolutionized marketing by giving businesses the ability to communicate directly with their target audience. It allows for immediate interaction and creates a personal connection between the company and the customer. Through social media, businesses can effectively spread their messages, get customer feedback, and increase their brand awareness.

One of the most important features of social media in marketing is the ability to spread content virally. When a company creates interesting and relevant content, it can be shared, liked, and commented on by users. As a result, the reach of the content can increase exponentially and the company can reach a larger number of potential customers.

In addition, social media offers companies the opportunity to better understand their target audience. By analyzing user data, businesses can gain valuable insights to improve their marketing strategies. They can analyze demographic information, interests, and behavioral patterns of their target audience and tailor their messages accordingly.

BENEFITS OF SOCIAL MEDIA IN MARKETING

The use of social media in marketing offers a variety of benefits for businesses. Here are some of the key benefits:

1. **Increased** brand awareness: By having a presence on social media platforms, businesses can increase their brand awareness and reach their target audience. By regularly sharing relevant content and interacting with their followers, they can increase awareness of their brand.
2. **Direct customer interaction**: Social media allows businesses to interact directly with their customers. Customers can ask questions, provide feedback, and share their opinions. This direct interaction creates a personal connection and builds customer trust in the brand.
3. **Increase** website traffic: By linking content on social media platforms, businesses can drive traffic to their website. By sharing interesting content and encouraging users to click on the link, they can drive more traffic to their website.
4. **Improved** customer retention: Social media allows businesses to improve their customer retention. By regularly sharing relevant content and interacting with their followers, they can maintain the interest and loyalty of their customers.
5. **Effective targeting**: Social media platforms offer advanced targeting options that allow businesses to accurately reach their target audience. By leveraging demographics, interests, and behavioral patterns, businesses can target their ads to the right people.

SUCCESS FACTORS FOR SOCIAL MEDIA MARKETING

For social media marketing to be successful, companies need to consider a few key success factors. Here are some tips to get the most out of social media marketing:

1. **Set** clear goals: Before companies start social media marketing, they should define clear goals. Do they want to increase brand awareness, increase sales, or improve customer retention? By setting clear goals, they can align their strategies accordingly.
2. **Choosing the** right platforms: Not all social media platforms are right for every business. Businesses should choose the platforms that best suit their target audience and marketing goals. It is important to understand the platforms and how to use them effectively.
3. **Create** high-quality content: To succeed on social media, businesses need to create high-quality content. The content should be relevant, interesting, and engaging. By providing valuable content, businesses can capture the interest of their target audience and increase their brand awareness.
4. **Regular activity**: To be successful on social media, it's important to be active on a regular basis. Businesses should regularly update their profiles, share content, and interact with their followers. By having a constant presence, companies can maintain the interest of their target audience.
5. **Monitoring and analytics**: Businesses should monitor and analyze their social media activity. You should track the performance of their posts, the engagement of their followers, and other relevant metrics. By analyzing this data, companies can optimize their strategies and achieve better results.

Social media has become an indispensable tool in marketing. It provides businesses with the opportunity to interact with their target audience, increase their brand awareness, and increase sales. By choosing the right platforms, creating high-quality content, and monitoring their activities, businesses can realize the full potential of social media marketing.

CHOOSING THE RIGHT SOCIAL MEDIA PLATFORMS

Choosing the right social media platforms is a crucial step for a successful social media marketing strategy. Each platform has its own characteristics, audiences, and functions to consider. In this section, we'll take a closer look at choosing the right platforms and help you make the best decisions for your business.

TARGET GROUP ANALYSIS

Before choosing a social media platform, it's important to know your target audience intimately. Who are your customers? What is their age range, interests, and demographics? What platforms are they already using? By answering these questions, you can identify the platforms where your target audience is most active.

PLATFORMS AT A GLANCE

There are a variety of social media platforms that cater to different audiences and features. Here are some of the most popular platforms at a glance:

Facebook

Facebook is the largest social media platform with over 2 billion active users worldwide. It offers a wide range of features, including sharing posts, photos, and videos, creating events, and connecting with friends and family. Facebook is suitable for businesses of all types and sizes because it has a large and diverse user base.

Instagram

Instagram is a visual platform that focuses on sharing photos and videos. It has over 1 billion active users and is especially popular with younger audiences. Instagram works well for businesses that have visually appealing content, such as fashion, travel, food, and lifestyle.

Twitter

Twitter is a platform where users can post short messages, called tweets. It has over 330 million active users and is known for its real-time communication and ability to network with influencers and experts in various industries. Twitter is a good fit for businesses that want to share up-to-date information and are looking for a wide reach.

LinkedIn

LinkedIn is a social network for professional contacts and business initiation. It has over 700 million members worldwide and is especially popular among professionals and businesses. LinkedIn is a good fit for B2B companies and those that focus on professional services and career development.

YouTube

YouTube is a video platform where users can upload, watch, and share videos. It has over 2 billion monthly active users and is the second largest search engine in the world. YouTube is a good fit for businesses that have visual content and want to engage their target audience with videos.

PLATFORM SELECTION BASED ON GOALS AND RESOURCES

When choosing the right social media platforms, you should also consider your goals and resources. What goals do you want to achieve with your social media strategy? Do you want to raise awareness of your brand, generate leads, or increase sales? Depending on your goals, certain platforms may be more suitable than others.

In addition, you should also consider your resources. How much time and staff can you devote to maintaining your social media presence? Some platforms require more effort and commitment than others. Make sure you have the resources to create high-quality content and interact with your target audience on a regular basis.

TEST & OPTIMIZE

Choosing the right social media platforms is not a one-time process. It is important to regularly check if the chosen platforms are delivering the desired results. Analyze the performance of your posts, the engagement of your target audience, and the number of conversions coming from each platform.

Based on this data, you can adjust your strategy and test new platforms if necessary. Be open to change and experiment with different platforms to see which ones best suit your business.

RESULT

Choosing the right social media platforms is an important step in a successful social media marketing strategy. By considering your target audience, goals, and resources, you can identify the platforms where you can best reach your target audience. Test regularly and tweak your strategy to make sure you're getting the best results.

CONTENT STRATEGY FOR SOCIAL MEDIA

An effective content strategy is crucial to the success of your social media marketing. By creating and distributing high-quality content, you can engage your target audience, pique their interest, and build long-term customer loyalty. In this section, we'll show you how to develop and implement a social media content strategy.

TARGET GROUP ANALYSIS

Before you start creating content, it's important to have a deep understanding of your target audience. A detailed audience analysis allows you to better understand the needs, interests, and preferences of your potential customers. This allows you to create content that is tailored to their specific needs and has a greater impact.

To get to know your target audience better, you can use different methods. One way is to conduct surveys or interviews to get direct feedback from your customers. You can also use social media and online analytics tools to gather information about your target audience's behavior and demographics.

CONTENT TYPES AND FORMATS

When creating your content strategy, you should consider different types and formats of content. This allows you to communicate your message in a variety of ways and capture the attention of your target audience.

Some popular types of content for social media include:

- Blog articles: Write informative and entertaining articles that interest your target audience.
- Infographics: Visualize complex information and data in an engaging way.
- Videos: Create short videos to showcase your products or services or provide how-to guides.
- Images and graphics: Use visual content to get your message across and grab attention.

- Surveys and quizzes: Offer interactive content to increase engagement with your target audience.

It's important to choose the right formats for your target audience and the particular social media platform. For example, short videos are popular for platforms like Instagram and TikTok, while longer videos can work better on YouTube.

CONTENT PLANNING & CREATION

Good content planning is key to the success of your content strategy. Create an editorial plan that specifies what content you want to publish, when, and on which platforms. This allows you to maintain a consistent and well-organized content stream.

When creating content, you should make sure that it is relevant, engaging, and of high quality. Make sure your content appeals to the needs and interests of your target audience and provides them with value. Use clear and understandable language and pay attention to spelling and grammar.

It can also be helpful to combine different media formats to get your message across more effectively. For example, you can complement a blog article with an infographic or short video to appeal to different learning styles and increase engagement with your target audience.

CONTENT DISTRIBUTION AND PROMOTION

Creating great content alone isn't enough. You also need to make sure that your content is seen by your target audience. Take advantage of the various features and tools offered by social media platforms to distribute and promote your content.

One way to spread your content is by using hashtags. Use relevant hashtags in your posts to increase your reach and be found by users searching for specific topics. You can also tag influencers or other relevant accounts to make your content accessible to a larger audience.

In addition, you can use paid advertising on social media platforms to promote your content in a targeted manner. Use targeting options to show your ads only to your target audience and maximize the effectiveness of your campaigns.

SUCCESS MEASUREMENT AND OPTIMISATION

To measure and optimize the success of your content strategy, it's important to track relevant metrics. Regularly monitor the performance of your content to see which content is performing well and which needs to be optimized.

Some key metrics to track include:

- Reach: How many people have seen your content?
- Engagement: How many likes, comments, and shares did your content generate?
- Clicks: How many people clicked on links in your posts?
- Conversion rate: How many people took a desired action after consuming your content?

Based on these metrics, you can optimize your content strategy by replicating successful content and improving or removing less successful content.

RESULT

A well-thought-out content strategy is crucial to the success of your social media marketing. By creating and distributing high-quality content, you can engage your target audience, pique their interest, and build long-term customer loyalty. Use the tips and methods presented in this section to develop and implement your own social media content strategy.

COMMUNITY MANAGEMENT & CUSTOMER ENGAGEMENT

Community management and customer retention are two crucial aspects of social media marketing. A well-maintained community can not only increase brand awareness, but also strengthen customer loyalty and ultimately lead to more sales. In this section, we'll take a closer look at the strategies and techniques of community management and customer engagement in digital marketing.

THE IMPORTANCE OF COMMUNITY MANAGEMENT

Community management refers to managing and maintaining a brand's or company's online community. An active and engaged community can be a valuable resource for improving brand image and gaining customer trust. Through community management, businesses can establish direct interactions with their customers, collect feedback, and respond to questions or issues.

A well-maintained community can also serve as a mouthpiece for the company to introduce new products or services, announce events, or just keep in touch with customers. By building a strong community, businesses can build a loyal following that is willing to support and recommend their brand to others.

CHOOSING THE RIGHT COMMUNITY MANAGEMENT PLATFORM

Choosing the right community management platform is crucial to achieving the desired results. There are a variety of social media platforms that can be used for community management, including Facebook, Twitter, Instagram, LinkedIn, and many more. Each platform has its own advantages and disadvantages, and it's important to consider the company's target audience and goals.

Facebook is one of the most popular platforms for community management because it has a large user base and offers a variety of features to interact with the community. Twitter is good for real-time communication and sharing short messages or updates. Instagram is ideal for visual content and sharing images and videos. LinkedIn, on the other hand, is more geared towards professional networks and is well suited for B2B companies.

It's important to choose the platforms where the company's target audience spends the most time. A thorough audience analysis can help identify the right platforms for community management.

ACTIVELY ENGAGE THE COMMUNITY

To build an active and engaged community, it's important to share content and interact with followers on a regular basis. Businesses should create relevant and engaging content that appeals to the interests and needs of the target audience. This can be in the form of blog articles, videos, infographics, or other formats.

It's also important to respond to comments, questions, and feedback from the community. By responding quickly and professionally, companies can build customer trust and show that they care about their concerns. Sharing user-generated content can also be an effective way to engage the community and increase engagement.

In addition, companies can also host special promotions or contests to motivate and reward the community. This may include, for example, the raffle of prizes, exclusive discounts or the opportunity to participate in events.

CUSTOMER LOYALTY THROUGH COMMUNITY MANAGEMENT

Community management can also help build customer loyalty. By building an engaged community, businesses can build a personal relationship with their customers and build trust. Customers who feel connected to a brand are more likely to shop with it repeatedly and recommend it to others.

One way to drive customer loyalty through community management is to provide exclusive offers or discounts to community members. This can help reward customer loyalty and encourage them to continue to stay in touch with the company.

In addition, companies can also use customer feedback to improve their products or services. By catering to customers' needs and wants, businesses can ensure that they are satisfying their customers and building long-term relationships.

MEASURING SUCCESS IN COMMUNITY MANAGEMENT

Measuring success in community management is crucial to evaluate the effectiveness of the strategies used and to make improvements. There are several metrics that businesses can track to measure the success of their community management.

An important metric is the number of followers or members of the community. A growing community can indicate that the company is successful in attracting new customers and maintaining the interest of existing customers.

Engagement rate is another important metric that indicates how active the community is. This can be measured by the number of likes, comments, shares, or other interactions. A high engagement rate indicates that the community appreciates the company's content and is willing to engage with it.

In addition, companies can also track sales or conversion rate to measure the impact of community management on business success. By tracking revenue or the number of sales generated by the community, businesses can determine if their community strategies are effective.

RESULT

Community management and customer retention are crucial aspects of digital marketing. By building an engaged community, businesses can gain customer trust, increase brand awareness, and ultimately increase sales. By choosing the right platforms, actively engaging the community, and strengthening customer loyalty, businesses can build long-term relationships with their customers and succeed in digital marketing.

CONTENT MARKETING

FUNDAMENTALS OF CONTENT MARKETING

Content marketing is one of the most important strategies in digital marketing. It's all about creating and distributing high-quality and relevant content to capture the attention and interest of the target audience. Through targeted content marketing, businesses can increase brand awareness, better reach their target audience, and ultimately increase sales.

WAS IST CONTENT MARKETING?

Content marketing refers to the creation and distribution of content that is relevant and valuable to the target audience. It's about offering information, entertainment, or solutions to problems that the target audience has. The content can be created in various formats such as blog articles, videos, infographics, ebooks, or social media posts.

The goal of content marketing is to build trust and credibility by providing valuable information. By providing relevant content, businesses can better engage their target audience and build a long-term relationship.

WHY IS CONTENT MARKETING IMPORTANT?

Content marketing is important because it allows businesses to stand out from the competition and effectively target their target audience. Here are some reasons why content marketing plays an important role in digital marketing:

1. **Increase brand awareness**: By creating high-quality content, businesses can spread the word about their brand

and reach their target audience. If the content is relevant and valuable, people will be more likely to share and recommend it to others.

2. **Building** trust and credibility: By providing valuable information, companies can gain the trust and credibility of their target audience. If the target audience feels that the company has in-depth knowledge and expertise, they are more likely to buy products or services from that company.

3. **Generating** qualified leads: By creating content that is tailored to the needs and interests of the target audience, businesses can generate qualified leads. If the target audience finds the content relevant, they are more likely to leave their contact details and receive more information from the company.

4. **Improving search engine ranking**: Search engines like Google prefer high-quality and relevant content. By creating high-quality content on a regular basis, businesses can improve their search engine rankings and attract more organic traffic to their website.

5. **Strengthen** customer loyalty: By providing continuous and relevant content, businesses can strengthen customer loyalty. If the target audience finds the content useful and interesting, they will be more likely to stay loyal to the company and buy products or services repeatedly.

THE CONTENT MARKETING STRATEGY

A successful content marketing strategy requires careful planning and execution. Here are the steps to keep in mind when developing a content marketing strategy:

1. **Objective**: Define clear goals for your content marketing strategy. Do you want to increase brand awareness, generate qualified leads, or improve customer retention?

2. **Audience analysis**: Analyze your audience to better understand their needs, interests, and preferences. This

helps you create content that is tailored to their specific needs.

3. **Content planning**: Develop a detailed plan for content creation and publishing. Consider the type of content, format, schedule, and channels through which the content will be distributed.
4. **Content creation**: Create high-quality and relevant content that meets the needs of your target audience. Make sure the content is well-researched, well-written, and attractively designed.
5. **Content distribution**: Distribute your content through various channels such as your website, social media platforms, email marketing, and other relevant channels. Make sure the content is optimized for each channel.
6. **Measurement and optimization**: Monitor the performance of your content and analyze the results. Identify which content is performing well and which needs to be optimized for better results.

A well-thought-out content marketing strategy can help your business succeed in digital marketing. It's important to continuously create and distribute high-quality and relevant content to capture the attention and interest of your target audience.

CONTENT STRATEGY & PLANNING

Content strategy is a crucial part of digital marketing. It determines what type of content should be created to appeal to the target audience and achieve marketing goals. A well-thought-out content strategy can help increase brand visibility, strengthen customer loyalty, and ultimately increase sales.

OBJECTIVE OF THE CONTENT STRATEGY

Before you start creating content, it's important to set clear goals for your content strategy. These goals should be specific,

measurable, achievable, relevant, and time-bound. Possible targets
could be:

- Increase brand awareness
- Generation of qualified leads
- Increase in website traffic
- Improve customer retention
- Positioning as an expert in the industry

By defining clear goals, you can target your content strategy and
measure the success of your efforts.

TARGET GROUP ANALYSIS

To create effective content, it's important to know your target
audience intimately. A thorough audience analysis will help you
understand the needs, interests, and preferences of your potential
customers. You can use different methods to gather information
about your target audience, such as surveys, interviews, or
analyzing customer data.

Based on the insights gained, you can design your content to
address the needs of your target audience and provide them with
value. By creating relevant and engaging content, you can pique
the interest of your target audience and get them to interact with
your brand.

CONTENT TYPES AND FORMATS

When creating a content strategy, it's important to consider
different types and formats of content. Depending on the target
audience and marketing goals, different content can be effective.
Here are some popular content types and formats:

- Blog articles: Blog articles are a great way to share
  informative and entertaining content. You can focus on

different topics that are relevant to your target audience and provide them with valuable information.

- Infographics: Infographics are visual representations of information and data. They are an effective way to present complex information in an easy-to-understand and engaging way.
- Videos: Videos are one of the most popular forms of content in digital marketing. You can create different types of videos, such as explainer videos, product launches, or interviews. Videos have a high viral reach and can increase the engagement of your target audience.
- E-books: E-books are more extensive content that is presented in a PDF format. They can provide detailed information on a specific topic and can be used as a lead magnet to collect email addresses from potential customers.
- Social media posts: Social media posts are short and concise pieces of content that can be shared on platforms like Facebook, Twitter, or Instagram. You can use different formats, such as text, images, or videos, to get your message across.
- Podcasts: Podcasts are audio content that can be streamed or downloaded on various platforms. They offer a great way to share information and stories in a fun and informative way.

By using different types and formats of content, you can engage your target audience and grab their attention in different ways.

CONTENT PLANNING & CREATION

An effective content strategy requires careful planning and organization. A content plan will help you plan your content ahead of time and make sure it's published regularly. Here are some steps to keep in mind when planning and creating content:

1. Establish an editorial calendar: An editorial calendar is a tool that helps you plan and organize your content in

advance. You can specify what type of content to publish and when, and make sure you create new content on a regular basis.
2. Keyword research: Before you start creating content, it's important to do thorough keyword research. This will help you identify relevant keywords that should be used in your content to increase search engine visibility.
3. Creating high-quality content: When creating content, it's important to deliver high-quality and relevant content. Make sure your content is well-researched, well-written, and attractively designed.
4. Consider different channels: When creating content, remember to consider different channels that your target audience is active on. Tailor your content to the needs and specifics of these channels for maximum impact.
5. Publish scheduling: Carefully plan the publication of your content to ensure it is available in the right place at the right time. You should also consider seasonal or current events that may be relevant to your target audience.

By carefully planning and organizing your content, you can ensure that your message is communicated effectively and your marketing goals are met.

CONTENT-DISTRIBUTION

Creating high-quality content is just the first step. To reach your target audience, it's important to distribute your content effectively. Here are some ways you can successfully distribute your content:

- Social media marketing: Use social media platforms like Facebook, Twitter, Instagram, or LinkedIn to share your content and reach your target audience. Use relevant hashtags to increase the visibility of your posts.

- Email marketing: Use your email list to send your content to your subscribers. Make sure your emails are attractively designed and provide clear value.
- Influencer marketing: Work with influencers who target your target audience to share your content and increase your reach.
- Guest posting: Write guest posts for other websites or blogs to get your content in front of a new audience and generate backlinks.
- Search Engine Optimization: Optimize your content for search engines to generate organic traffic to your website. Use relevant keywords, optimize your meta tags, and improve your website's loading speed.

By using different distribution channels, you can ensure that your content is seen and consumed by your target audience.

SUCCESS MEASUREMENT AND OPTIMISATION

Measuring success is an important part of your content strategy. By measuring the success of your content, you can determine what type of content is most effective and what optimizations need to be made. Here are some metrics to consider when measuring success:

- Website traffic: Monitor the number of visitors to your website to see how well your content is performing.
- Engagement: Measure the engagement of your target group, e.g. by the number of likes, comments

CONTENT CREATION & DISTRIBUTION

The creation and distribution of high-quality content is a crucial success factor in digital marketing. In this section, we'll look at how to create engaging and relevant content and distribute it effectively to reach and engage your target audience.

THE IMPORTANCE OF HIGH-QUALITY CONTENT

In an age where information is abundant, it's crucial to create high-quality content that stands out from the crowd. Your content should be informative, relevant, and engaging to capture your audience's interest and inspire them to take action.

High-quality content gives you the opportunity to demonstrate your expertise and credibility and convince your target audience. By providing valuable information, you can gain the trust of your readers and build long-term relationships.

FINDING CONTENT-IDEAS

Finding new and interesting content ideas can be challenging. Here are some strategies that can help you come up with inspiring ideas for your content:

- Conduct a comprehensive audience analysis to better understand your audience's needs, interests, and pain points. This allows you to create targeted content that addresses these needs.
- Regularly review the trends and developments in your industry. Read technical articles, attend conferences, and connect with other experts to stay up-to-date.
- Analyze your competitors' content. Identify which topics work well and which gaps you can fill.
- Ask your customers and readers about their interests and challenges. Use surveys, feedback, and comments to gain insights and adjust your content strategy.

CONTENT-ERSTELLUNG

Creating high-quality content takes time, effort, and creativity. Here are some best practices that can help you create engaging content:

- Define clear goals for your content. Do you want to inform, entertain or inspire? Make sure your content is aligned with these goals.
- Use clear and understandable language. Avoid jargon and make sure your content is accessible to your target audience.
- Structure your content well. Use headings, paragraphs, and bulleted lists to make your content easy to read and understand.
- Use different formats to diversify your content. Use text, images, videos, infographics, and other media to get your message across.
- Make sure it is attractively designed. Use high-quality images, matching colors, and clear formatting to present your content in a visually appealing way.

CONTENT-DISTRIBUTION

Distributing your content is just as important as creating it. Here are some strategies to distribute your content effectively:

- Use social media platforms to share your content and increase your reach. Identify the platforms where your audience spends most of their time and tailor your content accordingly.
- Publish regular blog posts on your own website or guest blogs to demonstrate your expertise and generate traffic.
- Use email marketing to send your content directly to your subscribers. Create engaging newsletters and inform your readers about new content, offers, and events.
- Collaborate with influencers and other industry experts to bring your content to a wider audience.
- Use SEO strategies to optimize your content for search engines and generate organic traffic.

SUCCESS MEASUREMENT AND OPTIMISATION

Regularly measuring and optimizing your content marketing efforts is critical to maximizing the success of your efforts. Here are some key metrics to keep an eye on:

- Pageviews and unique visitors: These metrics give you insight into how many people see your content and how popular it is.
- Dwell time: Dwell time on your website tells you how engaged your visitors are and how well your content keeps them interested.
- Social media interactions: Check how often your content is shared, liked, and commented on to see how well it resonates with your target audience.
- Conversion rate: Measure how many visitors to your website actually take a desired action, such as making a purchase or filling out a contact form.
- Feedback and comments: Take your readers' feedback seriously and use it to continuously improve your content.

By regularly analyzing your metrics and adjusting your content strategy accordingly, you can ensure that your content is successful and meets your marketing goals.

RESULT

Creating and distributing high-quality content is an essential part of a successful digital marketing strategy. By creating relevant and engaging content and distributing it effectively, you can reach your target audience, earn their trust, and build long-term relationships. Don't forget to measure and optimize your content marketing efforts regularly to maximize the success of your efforts.

CONTENT OPTIMIZATION & MEASUREMENT

Content optimization and measurement are crucial steps in content marketing. By continuously improving and monitoring your content, you can ensure that it is effective and achieving the desired results. In this section, we'll take a closer look at content optimization and measurement, and give you practical tips on how to improve your content.

THE IMPORTANCE OF CONTENT OPTIMIZATION

Content optimization refers to customizing and improving your content to make it more attractive to search engines and users. By optimizing your content, you can improve your website's visibility in search engine results and attract more qualified visitors. In addition, by optimizing your content, you can improve the user experience and ensure that your content is relevant and engaging.

KEYWORD OPTIMIZATION

Keyword optimization is an important part of content optimization. By selecting and integrating relevant keywords into your content, you can ensure that your content is recognized by search engines and displayed in search results. It's important to place your keywords strategically and incorporate them naturally into your content. Avoid keyword stuffing, as it can be considered spam by search engines.

ON-PAGE OPTIMIZATION

On-page optimization refers to the optimization of the individual pages of your website. This is all about making your content more accessible and user-friendly to search engines and users. Some of the important aspects of on-page optimization include optimizing the page title, meta description, headings, URL structure, and internal linking. Make sure your content is well-structured and easy to understand.

OPTIMIZATION OF IMAGES AND VIDEOS

Images and videos are important elements of content marketing. You can make your content more visually appealing and informative. When optimizing images and videos, it's important that you optimize the file size to improve your website's loading time. Use relevant file names, alt tags, and descriptions to ensure that your images and videos can be recognized and indexed by search engines.

A/B TESTING AND CONVERSION OPTIMIZATION

A/B testing is an effective way to measure and improve the performance of your content. By testing different versions of your content, you can find out which version works better and gets the results you want. A/B testing can be done on various elements such as headlines, call-to-actions, color schemes, and layouts. By running A/B tests, you can continuously optimize your content and improve the conversion rate.

ANALYSIS AND PERFORMANCE MEASUREMENT

Analysis and performance measurement are crucial to measuring and understanding the success of your content. By using web analytics tools like Google Analytics, you can measure key metrics like page views, dwell time, bounce rate, and conversion rate. This data can give you valuable insights into your users' behavior and help you further optimize your content. Be sure to regularly review your analytics data and make the necessary adjustments.

THE IMPORTANCE OF QUALITATIVE FEEDBACK

Qualitative feedback from users and customers is a valuable resource to improve your content. Ask your users for feedback on your content and take their suggestions and suggestions seriously. By taking qualitative feedback into account, you can tailor your content to the needs and expectations of your target audience and ensure that it is relevant and engaging.

THE CONTINUOUS OPTIMISATION OF YOUR CONTENT

Optimizing your content is a continuous process. It's important to regularly review, analyze, and optimize your content to ensure it's effective and getting the results you want. Take the time to revise your content, come up with new ideas, and adjust your strategy. By continuously optimizing your content, you can be successful in digital marketing in the long term.

In this section, we've looked at content optimization and measurement in digital marketing. We've highlighted the importance of content optimization and provided practical tips on how to improve your content. In addition, we emphasized the importance of analysis and performance measurement and discussed the role of qualitative feedback. By continuously optimizing your content, you can ensure that it is effective and achieves the desired results.

EMAIL MARKETING AND NEWSLETTERS

EMAIL MARKETING AS AN EFFECTIVE MARKETING TOOL

Email marketing is one of the oldest yet most effective forms of digital marketing. It allows businesses to communicate directly with their customers and send personalized messages. In this section, we'll take a closer look at the benefits of email marketing, building an email list, segmenting contacts, creating and sending email campaigns, and measuring and optimizing success in email marketing.

BENEFITS OF EMAIL MARKETING

Email marketing offers a variety of benefits for businesses. First, it is cost-effective compared to other marketing channels. Businesses can send large volumes of emails at a relatively low cost. Second, email marketing allows for direct communication with customers. Businesses can send personalized messages and thus build a closer relationship with their customers. Third, email marketing is measurable. Businesses can accurately track the success of their email campaigns using metrics such as open rate, click-through rate, and conversion rate. Finally, email marketing is also very effective because most people check their emails regularly, so there is a high chance that the messages will be seen.

BUILDING AN EMAIL LIST AND SEGMENTATION

Before businesses can start sending email campaigns, they need to build an email list. There are several ways to do this. One way is to offer a newsletter sign-up form on the company's website. Customers can provide their email address and receive regular updates and offers via email. Another option is to ask existing customers to sign up for the newsletter when they make a purchase or use a service. In addition, businesses can also use social media channels to grow their email list, for example by offering exclusive content or discounts for those who sign up for the newsletter.

Once an email list is built, it's important to segment the contacts. This means dividing the contacts into different groups based on criteria such as demographics, buying behavior, or interests. Segmentation allows businesses to send more targeted and relevant messages to their customers, increasing the likelihood that they will be opened and clicked.

CREATE AND SEND EMAIL CAMPAIGNS

When creating email campaigns, it's important for businesses to deliver engaging and relevant content. The subject line should grab the recipient's attention and make them curious to open the newsletter. The content of the email should be informative, useful, and engaging. For example, companies can send new products, exclusive offers, informative articles, or personalized recommendations. In addition, emails should also include a clear call-to-action that encourages the recipient to click on a link, make a purchase, or sign up for an event.

Before companies send out their email campaigns, it's wise to test them. This means that they send the emails to a small group of recipients and review the results before sending them to the entire email list. By testing, businesses can ensure that their emails are displayed correctly, that all links work, and that the messages are clearly conveyed.

MEASURING AND OPTIMISING SUCCESS IN EMAIL MARKETING

Measuring success in email marketing is crucial to evaluate the effectiveness of campaigns and identify areas for improvement. Businesses can track various metrics to measure the success of their email campaigns. This includes the open rate, click-through rate, conversion rate, and unsubscribe rate. By analyzing these metrics, businesses can determine which emails are performing well and which need to be optimized.

In order to continuously improve email marketing, it is important to conduct regular A/B testing. It involves creating two versions of an email and sending it to different groups of recipients. By comparing the results, companies can determine which version works better and which elements can be optimized.

To sum up, email marketing is an extremely effective marketing tool. It allows businesses to communicate directly with their customers and send personalized messages. By building an email list, segmenting contacts, creating and sending engaging email campaigns, and measuring and optimizing success, businesses can realize the full potential of email marketing and achieve their marketing goals.

BUILDING AN EMAIL LIST AND SEGMENTATION

A well-built email list is a valuable asset for any digital marketing business. It allows you to communicate directly with your prospects and provide them with relevant information. But how do you build an email list and segment it to target the right audience? In this section, we will show you how to build and segment an effective email list.

THE IMPORTANCE OF AN EMAIL LIST

An email list is a collection of email addresses of potential customers who have voluntarily opted in to receive information from your company. It is a valuable tool for sending your marketing messages to your target audience. Compared to other marketing channels, email marketing offers a high reach and a personal approach.

BUILDING AN EMAIL LIST

To build an email list, you need to motivate potential customers to share their email address with you. Here are some best practices to achieve this:

1. Landing pages: Create engaging landing pages on your website where visitors can leave their email address. Offer value such as a free download, ebook, or newsletter to increase conversions.
2. Pop-up windows: Use pop-up windows on your website to prompt visitors to sign up for your newsletter. Make sure that the pop-up window is attractively designed and provides clear value.
3. Social media: Use your social media presence to invite potential customers to sign up for your newsletter. Publish regular posts that point out your newsletter and provide an incentive to sign up.
4. Sweepstakes & Promotions: Run sweepstakes or promotions that require participants to leave their email address in order to participate. This is an effective way to quickly collect a large number of email addresses.

EMAIL LIST SEGMENTATION

Once you've built an email list, it's important to segment it to send your marketing messages to the right audience. Here are some ways you can segment your email list:

1. Demographics: Segment your list based on demographics such as age, gender, location, or income. This allows you to send targeted marketing messages to different audiences.
2. Buying behavior: Segment your list based on your customers' buying behavior. Divide your customers into categories such as new customers, existing customers or frequent buyers and send them customized offers accordingly.

3. Interests and preferences: Collect information about your customers' interests and preferences and segment your list accordingly. Send personalized content and offers tailored to your customers' individual needs and interests.
4. Open and click behavior: Analyze the open and click behavior of your subscribers and segment your list based on their engagement. Send targeted follow-up emails to those who regularly open your emails and click on links.

PRIVACY & CONSENT

When building and using your email list, it's important to comply with privacy regulations and get consent from your subscribers. Make sure you're transparent about the type of information you're going to send, and give your subscribers the option to unsubscribe at any time.

RESULT

A well-built and segmented email list is a valuable tool in digital marketing. It allows you to send targeted marketing messages to your target audience and build a personal relationship with your potential customers. Use the different methods to build your email list and segment it to optimize your marketing strategy. Always remember to comply with privacy regulations and get consent from your subscribers.

CREATE AND SEND EMAIL CAMPAIGNS

Email marketing is one of the most effective methods in digital marketing to connect with potential customers and inform them about news, offers, and other relevant information. In this section, we're going to look at how to create and send successful email campaigns.

PLANNING THE EMAIL CAMPAIGN

Before you start creating and sending your email campaign, it's important to have a clear strategy and plan. Here are some steps to keep in mind when planning your email campaign:

1. Define your goals: Think about what you want to achieve with your email campaign. Do you want to increase sales, attract new customers or improve customer loyalty? By setting clear goals, you can better align your campaign with those goals.
2. Determine your target audience: Identify your target audience and segment them to provide relevant content and offers. The better you know your target audience, the more targeted you can make your email campaign.
3. Create a schedule: Decide when and how often you want to send your emails. Be careful not to send emails too often or too infrequently so as not to overload or neglect your subscribers.
4. Develop a content strategy: Think about what kind of content you want to include in your emails. This can be informative articles, product announcements, discount promotions, or exclusive content. Make sure your content is relevant and engaging to your target audience.

THE CREATION OF THE EMAIL CAMPAIGN

Now that you've planned your email campaign, it's time to create it. Here are some important steps to keep in mind when creating your email campaign:

1. Choose a responsive design: Design your emails to look professional and engaging. Use a responsive design that adapts to different screen sizes, as many people read emails on their mobile devices.
2. Use a clear and compelling subject line: The subject line is the first thing your subscribers see, so it's important that it's

clear and compelling. Use a subject line that piques interest and encourages them to open the email.

3. Personalize your emails: Personalization is an important aspect of email marketing. Use the recipient's name in the salutation and tailor the content of the email to the recipient's interests and preferences.

4. Add a call-to-action: Each email should include a clear call-to-action that prompts the recipient to take a specific action. This could be buying a product, filling out a form, or visiting your website.

SENDING THE E-MAIL CAMPAIGN

Now that you've created your email campaign, it's time to send it. Here are some important steps to keep in mind when sending your email campaign:

1. Use a reliable email marketing tool: There are many email marketing tools on the market that can help you send out your email campaign. Choose a reliable tool that gives you features like creating email templates, managing subscriber lists, and tracking campaign statistics.

2. Test your emails before you send them: Before you send your emails to your subscribers, you should make sure they look great on different devices and email clients. Run tests to make sure your emails are displayed correctly and all links and images are working.

3. Monitor the performance of your email campaign: Track the open and click-through rates of your emails to measure the performance of your campaign. Analyze the data and make adjustments if necessary to improve the effectiveness of your email campaign.

4. Provide an easy way to unsubscribe: Make sure your emails include an easy way to unsubscribe. Not only is this required by law, but it's also important to ensure that your

subscribers only receive emails they actually want to receive.

Email campaigns can be an extremely effective digital marketing tool to connect with your target audience and achieve your marketing goals. By developing a clear strategy, creating engaging emails, and monitoring how they are sent, you can create and send successful email campaigns.

MEASURING AND OPTIMISING SUCCESS IN EMAIL MARKETING

Email marketing is an extremely effective way to connect with your target audience and achieve your marketing goals. It allows you to send personalized messages to your subscribers and keep them updated on news, offers, and events. But how can you measure and optimize the success of your email campaigns? In this section, we'll look at the most important metrics and optimization techniques in email marketing.

OPEN RATE

Open rate is one of the most important metrics in email marketing. It indicates how many recipients have opened your email. A high open rate shows that your subject line and preview were successful and piqued the interest of recipients. To improve the open rate, you should use descriptive and engaging subject lines. Test different variants to see which ones work best.

CTR

The click-through rate measures how many recipients clicked on links in your email. A high click-through rate shows that your content is relevant and engaging. To increase click-through rates, use clear call-to-action buttons and provide clear value to recipients. Personalized content and exclusive offers can also help increase click-through rates.

CONVERSION RATE

Conversion rate is one of the most important metrics in email marketing. It indicates how many recipients have taken a desired action after opening your email, e.g. made a purchase or signed up for a newsletter. To improve the conversion rate, you should convey a clear and compelling message and incentivize recipients to take the desired action. An easy-to-use landing page and a simple checkout process can also help boost conversions.

UNSUBSCRIBE RATE

The unsubscribe rate is how many recipients have unsubscribed from your mailing list. A high unsubscribe rate can indicate that your content isn't relevant or too frequent. To reduce the unsubscribe rate, you should make sure that you only send relevant content to your subscribers and that the frequency of your emails is appropriate. Also, offer recipients the ability to adjust their email preferences to better accommodate their interests.

A/B-TESTING

A/B testing is an effective way to optimize the performance of your email campaigns. It involves creating two or more variations of an email and sending them to different segments of your audience. By comparing the results, you can find out which variant works better and optimize your emails accordingly. Test different elements such as subject lines, call-to-action buttons, content, and layouts for the best results.

AUTOMATION AND PERSONALIZATION

Automating and personalizing email campaigns can increase the effectiveness and relevance of your messages. By using marketing automation tools, you can send personalized emails based on your subscribers' behavior and interests. Segment your email list based on demographics, buying behavior, or interactions to offer relevant content. Personalized emails have a higher chance of being opened and clicked.

EMAIL MARKETING PLATFORMS & TOOLS

There are a variety of email marketing platforms and tools that can help you measure and optimize your email campaigns. These tools offer features such as A/B testing, automation, segmentation, and in-depth analytics. Examples of popular email marketing platforms include Mailchimp, Constant Contact, and Sendinblue. Choose a platform that meets your needs and gives you the necessary features to achieve your email marketing goals.

PRIVACY & LEGAL

When it comes to email marketing, it's important to comply with applicable privacy regulations and legal regulations. Make sure you have your subscribers' consent before sending them emails. Provide an easy way to unsubscribe and respect the privacy of your recipients. Find out about the applicable data protection laws in your country and follow email marketing best practices.

RESULT

Measuring success and optimizing in email marketing are crucial to making your email campaigns effective and achieving your marketing goals. By regularly monitoring and analyzing the relevant metrics, you can continuously improve your emails and increase engagement with your target audience. Use A/B testing, automation, and personalization to optimize your email campaigns and offer relevant content. Always pay attention to data protection and comply with the legal provisions ein.si

MOBILE MARKETING & APP MARKETING

THE IMPORTANCE OF MOBILE MARKETING

In today's digital world, the smartphone has become an indispensable companion. People use their mobile devices not only to make phone calls, but also to browse the web, shop, read the news, and connect with others through social media. This increasing use of mobile devices has made mobile marketing one of the most important strategies in digital marketing.

DIE MOBILE REVOLUTION

The proliferation of smartphones has sparked a real revolution in the way people access the internet. More and more people are using their mobile devices to get online, neglecting traditional desktop computers. This trend has led to companies having to adapt their marketing strategies and focus more on mobile marketing.

THE BENEFITS OF MOBILE MARKETING

Mobile marketing offers a variety of benefits for businesses. Firstly, it allows direct access to the customers, as most people carry their smartphones with them all the time. This means that companies can reach their target audience anytime and anywhere. Second, mobile marketing makes it possible to address customers in a personalized way. By using location data and other information, businesses can create tailored offers and promotional messages tailored to customers' individual needs and preferences. Thirdly, mobile marketing offers the opportunity to create interactive and engaging content. By integrating videos, images, and other interactive elements, businesses can build a deeper connection with their customers and increase their engagement.

MOBILE WEBSITES & APPS

To be successful in mobile marketing, businesses need to ensure that their websites and apps are optimized for mobile devices. A mobile website should load quickly, be user-friendly, and have a responsive design that automatically adjusts to the screen size of the device. In addition, businesses should ensure that their apps run smoothly and have useful features that provide value to users.

MOBILE ADVERTISING

Mobile advertising is an important part of mobile marketing. Businesses can use different types of mobile advertising formats to reach their target audience. These include banner ads, interstitial ads, video ads, and native ads. It's important for businesses to adapt their advertising messages to the specifics of the mobile medium and ensure that their ads are engaging and not intrusive.

MOBILE PAYMENTS

With the increasing use of mobile devices for online shopping, it's important for businesses to provide their customers with an easy and secure way to process payments through their mobile devices. Mobile payment solutions such as Apple Pay, Google Wallet and others allow customers to make their purchases conveniently and securely through their smartphones. Businesses should ensure that they integrate these payment methods into their e-commerce platforms to provide a frictionless shopping experience for their customers.

THE FUTURE OF MOBILE MARKETING

Mobile marketing will continue to play an important role in digital marketing in the future. With the ongoing development of technologies such as 5G and the increasing penetration of Internet of Things (IoT) devices, mobile usage will continue to grow. Businesses should therefore prepare to continuously adapt their mobile marketing strategies and develop innovative approaches to keep up with the changing needs and expectations of customers.

In this section, we have discussed the importance of mobile marketing in digital marketing. We have explained the benefits of mobile marketing for businesses and looked at the different aspects of mobile marketing such as mobile websites, apps, advertising, and payments. Finally, we provided an outlook on the future of mobile marketing and emphasized the importance for businesses to continuously adapt to changing mobile technologies and customer needs.

MOBILE OPTIMIZATION OF WEBSITES AND APPS

In today's digital world, mobile use of websites and apps is indispensable. More and more people are accessing the internet via their smartphones and tablets and expect an optimal user experience. Therefore, it is crucial for businesses to optimize their websites and apps for mobile devices in order to reach their target audience in the best possible way and increase the success of their digital marketing strategy.

THE IMPORTANCE OF MOBILE OPTIMIZATION

Mobile optimization of websites and apps is of great importance as the number of mobile internet users is steadily increasing. According to statistics, more than half of the world's internet users already use mobile devices to access the internet. This number is expected to continue to rise as smartphones and tablets become more powerful and affordable.

A website or app that isn't mobile-optimized can lead to a poor user experience, which in turn can lead to a high bounce rate and a loss of potential customers. A mobile-optimized website or app, on the other hand, offers users a user-friendly interface, fast loading times, and optimal display on different screen sizes. This helps to increase user engagement, increase time spent on the website or app, and ultimately increase the conversion rate.

THE MOST IMPORTANT ASPECTS OF MOBILE OPTIMIZATION

To achieve successful mobile optimization, companies should consider the following aspects:

Responsive Webdesign

Responsive web design is a technique in which the layout and content of a website automatically adapt to the screen size of the device. This ensures that the website looks its best on all devices, whether it's a smartphone, tablet, or desktop computer. Businesses should ensure that their websites have a responsive design to provide a consistent and user-friendly experience across all devices.

Mobile Navigation

Navigating a mobile website or app should be simple and intuitive. Since screen space is limited on mobile devices, it is important to place the navigation elements clearly and prominently. Companies should pay attention to clear and well-structured menu navigation to enable users to navigate easily.

Fast loading times

Mobile users often have less patience when it comes to loading websites or apps. Therefore, it is important that a mobile-optimized website or app loads quickly. Businesses should ensure that their websites and apps are optimized to minimize load times. This can be achieved by compressing images, reducing HTTP requests, and using caching techniques.

Mobile-friendly content

The content of a mobile website or app should be optimized for mobile use. This means that the texts should be easy to read without the user having to zoom or scroll. Images and videos should also be optimized for mobile viewing to ensure optimal display and fast loading times.

Mobile SEO

Mobile optimization also has an impact on search engine ranking. Search engines like Google favor mobile-optimized websites and apps and reward them with better rankings in search results. Businesses should therefore ensure that their websites and apps are optimized for mobile devices to improve their visibility in search engines.

MOBILE OPTIMIZATION BEST PRACTICES

To achieve successful mobile optimization, organizations should follow the following best practices:

- Use a responsive web design to ensure optimal display on all devices.
- Make sure navigating your mobile website or app is easy and intuitive.
- Optimize load times so as not to strain the patience of mobile users.
- Adapt your content for mobile use to ensure optimal readability and display.
- Pay attention to mobile SEO to improve your visibility in search engines.

By implementing these best practices, businesses can ensure that their websites and apps are optimized for mobile devices and provide an optimal user experience. This helps to increase user satisfaction, increase conversion rate, and ultimately maximize the success of their digital marketing strategy.

APP MARKETING STRATEGIES

The proliferation of smartphones and the increasing use of mobile apps have made app marketing an important part of digital marketing. To be successful in app marketing, it's crucial to develop a well-thought-out strategy. In this section, we will explore different app marketing strategies that can help you market your app successfully.

TARGET GROUP ANALYSIS

Before you start app marketing, it's important to have a deep understanding of your target audience. Analyze who your potential users are, what their needs are, and what kind of apps they prefer. Conduct market research to get an accurate picture of your target audience. This will help you effectively target your marketing strategy to your target audience.

APP STORE OPTIMIZATION (ASO)

One of the most important strategies in app marketing is App Store Optimization (ASO). ASO refers to optimizing your app listings on the app stores to improve your app's visibility and ranking. This includes selecting relevant keywords, optimizing app titles and descriptions, adding screenshots and videos, and collecting positive reviews and ratings. An effective ASO strategy can help your app be found better in app store search results and generate more downloads.

SOCIAL MEDIA MARKETING FOR APPS

Social media marketing is another important strategy to promote your app. Use social media platforms like Facebook, Instagram, Twitter, and LinkedIn to showcase your app and engage potential users. Create engaging content that resonates with your target audience and share it on your social media channels. Also, use paid advertising on social media platforms to increase your reach and attract more users to your app.

INFLUENCER-MARKETING

Influencer marketing can be an effective strategy to get your app in front of a wide audience. Identify influential people in your industry or niche and work with them to promote your app. Influencers can mention your app in their posts, write reviews, or even create tutorials to demonstrate your app's features. This can help gain the trust and interest of potential users and increase app downloads.

APP PARTNERSHIPS

Another strategy in app marketing is to collaborate with other apps or companies to increase your reach. Look for apps or businesses that have a similar audience to your app and suggest a partnership. For example, this could mean promoting your app in another app, or offering joint promotions or discounts. Through such partnerships, you can attract new users and spread the word about your app.

APP REVIEWS & RATINGS

Positive reviews and ratings play an important role in potential users' decision on whether or not to download your app. Actively ask your users for reviews and ratings, and make sure you act on feedback to gain users' trust. Also, use app review websites and blogs to introduce your app and get positive reviews. The more positive reviews and ratings your app has, the more likely users are to download it.

APP ANALYTICS & OPTIMIZATION

To measure and improve the success of your app marketing strategies, it's important to conduct regular app analytics. Use tools like Google Analytics or app analytics platforms to collect data about your app's usage. Analyze how users find your app, how they use it, and what features are popular. Based on these insights, you can optimize your app and make adjustments to improve the user experience and increase app downloads.

APP UPDATES AND CUSTOMER RETENTION

To retain your users in the long term and increase app usage, it's important to provide regular app updates. Listen to your users' feedback and add new features or improve existing ones. Regularly inform your users about app updates and offer incentives to continue using the app, such as exclusive content or discounts. Good customer retention is crucial to drive your app's growth in the long run.

These app marketing strategies can help you successfully market your app and attract more users. Experiment with different strategies and measure the results to see which ones work best for your app. Remember that app marketing is a continuous process and that it takes time and effort to achieve long-term success.

APP STORE OPTIMIZATION (ASO)

App Store Optimization (ASO) is a critical factor in the success of a mobile app. As the app market becomes more competitive, it is of great importance that your app is highly visible in the app stores and can be found by potential users. ASO is a set of measures aimed at improving your app's visibility and ranking in the app stores. In this section, we'll take a closer look at the different aspects of app store optimization.

CHOOSING THE RIGHT KEYWORDS

Choosing the right keywords is an important step in app store optimization. Keywords are the terms that users search for in the app stores to find apps. By incorporating relevant keywords into your app's title, description, and keywords, you can increase the likelihood that your app will appear in search results. It's important that the keywords you choose are both relevant and popular. There are various tools and techniques that can help you with keyword research and selection.

THE APP TITLE AND DESCRIPTION

The app title and description are two of the most important elements that will make potential users download your app. The app title should be concise, memorable, and meaningful. It should highlight the main feature or utility of your app. The description should provide detailed information about your app's features and benefits. You should also include relevant keywords in your app's title and description to improve visibility in search results.

APP RATINGS & RATINGS

App ratings and ratings play an important role in the ASO. Positive reviews and ratings can increase potential users' trust in your app and increase their willingness to download it. It's important to encourage your users to leave reviews and share their experiences with your app. You can achieve this through in-app pop-ups, reminders, or rewards. It's also important to respond to negative reviews and resolve issues to maintain user trust.

APP-ICONS UND SCREENSHOTS

The app icon and screenshots are the visuals that potential users first see when they come across your app. An engaging and well-designed app icon can pique users' interest and make them want to take a closer look at your app. The screenshots should illustrate the key features and benefits of your app. You should also highlight your app's interface and design. It's important that the app icon and screenshots look professional and reflect your app's brand.

APP UPDATES & OPTIMIZATION

Regular app updates are an important part of app store optimization. With regular updates, you can fix bugs, add new features, and improve your app's performance. It's important to listen to users' feedback and consider their needs. You should also monitor and optimize your app's performance to ensure that it runs smoothly and provides a good user experience. Regular updates and tweaks can help improve your app's ratings and ratings and increase visibility in the app stores.

APP PROMOTION & MARKETING

App store optimization alone may not be enough to ensure your app's success. It's important to actively promote and market your app to attract potential users. You can use various marketing channels such as social media, influencer marketing, app install ads, and PR to promote your app. It's also important to develop a clear marketing strategy and have a deep understanding of your target audience in order to run effective marketing campaigns.

App store optimization is a continuous process that requires regular monitoring, adjustment, and optimization. By implementing the above measures and continuously working on improving your app, you can increase your app's visibility, ranking, and success in the app stores.

MOBILE AD NETWORKS AND FORMATS

Mobile ad networks and formats play a crucial role in digital marketing. With the proliferation of smartphones and tablets, it has become imperative for businesses to align their advertising strategies with mobile devices. In this section, we'll look at the different types of mobile ad networks and formats and how they can be used effectively to increase the reach and success of your marketing campaigns.

MOBILE AD NETWORKS

Mobile ad networks are platforms that allow advertisers to show their ads on mobile websites and mobile apps. These networks connect advertisers with publishers who provide ad space on their mobile platforms. There are several types of mobile ad networks, including:

Search Networks

Search networks allow advertisers to show ads in the search results of mobile search engines. These ads are displayed based on the search terms entered and other factors. Search networks are an effective way to target targeted users who are actively searching for specific products or services.

Display Networks

Display networks offer advertisers the ability to run graphical ads on mobile apps and websites. These ads can appear in the form of banners, interactive ads, or video ads. Display networks offer broad reach and allow advertisers to reach their audience based on demographics, interests, and behaviors.

In-App Ad Networks

In-app ad networks allow advertisers to serve ads on mobile apps. These ads can appear in various formats such as banners, full-screen ads, or video ads. In-app ad networks provide an effective way to target users while they're using an app, allowing advertisers to target their ads based on demographics and behaviors.

MOBILE WERBEFORMATE

Mobile advertising formats encompass the different types of ads that can be displayed on mobile devices. Here are some of the most common mobile ad formats:

Banner Ads

Banner ads are static or animated ads that are placed at the top or bottom of a mobile website or app. They are usually rectangular and contain text and images. Banner ads are a popular form of mobile ads because they are easy to create and inexpensive.

Full-screen ads

Full-screen ads are ads that take up the entire screen of a mobile device. They provide an immersive experience and allow advertisers to present their message in an engaging and visually appealing way. Full-screen ads can appear in the form of images, videos, or interactive content.

Video Ads

Video ads are ads that play in the form of videos. They can appear before, during, or after videos are played on mobile apps or websites. Video ads are an effective way to grab users' attention and convey complex messages in a fun and informative way.

Native Ads

Native ads are ads that are seamlessly integrated into the content of a mobile app or website. They adapt to the design and functionality of the platform and provide a non-disruptive user experience. Native ads can appear in the form of articles, recommendations, or sponsored content.

TIPS FOR SUCCESSFUL MOBILE MARKETING

To unlock the full potential of mobile ad networks and formats, here are some tips for successful mobile marketing:

1. Audience Analysis: Understand your audience and their behavior on mobile devices to target your ads.
2. Mobile optimization: Make sure your website and ads are optimized for mobile devices to ensure a smooth user experience.
3. Creative design: Create engaging and visually appealing ads that grab users' attention.
4. Test and optimize: Run regular tests to monitor and optimize the performance of your ads.
5. Tracking and analytics: Use performance measurement and analysis tools to measure and improve the success of your mobile marketing campaigns.
6. Personalization: Use the power of personalization to deliver relevant and tailored content to your target audience.
7. Continuous development: Stay up-to-date with the latest trends and developments in mobile marketing and adjust your strategy accordingly.

By following these tips and making effective use of the various mobile ad networks and formats, you can expand your reach, engage your target audience, and increase the success of your marketing campaigns.

That was Section 8.5 on Mobile Ad Networks and Formats. In the next few sections, we'll look at other important aspects of digital marketing.